Betty Crocker's

Old-Fashioned Desserts

Betty Crocker's

Old-Fashioned Desserts

MACMILLAN • USA

Illustrations courtesy of Food and Drink: A Pictorial Archive from Nineteenth Century Source
Selected by Jim Harter. Dover Publications, Inc., New York.

IDG BOOKS WORLDWIDE, INC.

An International Data Group Company
919 E. Hillsdale Boulevard
Suite 400
Foster City, CA 94404

 The IDG Books Worldwide logo is a registered trademark
under exclusive license to IDG Books Worldwide, Inc.,
from International Data Group, Inc.

For general information on IDG Books Worldwide's books in the U.S., please call our Consumer
Customer Service department at 800-762-2974. For reseller information, including discounts and
premium sales, please call our Reseller Customer Service department at 800-434-3422.

Library of Congress Cataloging-in-Publication Data

Crocker, Betty.
  [Old-fashioned desserts]
  Betty Crocker's Old-fashioned desserts.
     p. cm.
  Includes index.
  ISBN 0-7645-6072-7
  1. Desserts   I. Title.   II. Title: Old-fashioned desserts.
TX773.C735   1992
641.8'6—dc20   91-15857
                                              CIP

For consistent baking results, the Betty Crocker Kitchens
recommend Gold Medal Flour.

Manufactured in the United States of America
10 9 8 7 6 5 4 3 2

First Edition

Contents

Introduction

Flaky pastries, creamy custard, decadent chocolate cake, simple fruit cobblers, chewy cookies . . . old-fashioned desserts are endlessly appealing. Names like roly-poly, slump, Petticoat Tails (page 100), pandowdy, flummery and jumbles bring us back to the warming memories of long-ago days. Perhaps you remember your grandmother stirring up some of these at the old kitchen table, and enjoying them with a big glass of ice-cold milk on a Sunday visit. Now you can make them yourself with this extraordinary, easy-to-use collection of mouthwatering, all-time favorite desserts. These are the desserts that we savor with pleasure, recall with love and long to share with family and friends.

Recipes of years past did not look just as they do today. As a matter of fact, it's difficult sometimes to imagine being able to use them; for example, instead of one cup of water, a recipe might have called for one sherry glass of water! Recipes once instructed "bake in a quick oven" instead of providing a temperature and a baking time. We have included a handful of our favorite old General Mills recipes (see pages viii–ix) so you can see what they used to look like. It's fun to see how things have changed . . . and how much they've stayed the same.

Reminiscing about the days when we were pampered with these delicious desserts, we have put together a collection of the very best old-fashioned recipes to share with you. Turn through the pages and feel confident that you're cooking with Betty Crocker—America's most trusted friend in the kitchen for more than sixty-five years. You will find sweet echoes of the past here: of quilting parties, New England town meetings, southern teas, boating parties and Victorian propriety. Come join us in our unabashedly nostalgic celebration of the recipes that have withstood the most important test—the test of time.

THE BETTY CROCKER EDITORS

Burnt Sugar Chiffon Cake (page 39), Streusel Peach Tarts (page 56), Peppermint Pinwheels (page 101)

DESSERTS
THEN

☞In 1910 we published The Gold Medal Flour Cook Book, one of our very first cookbooks. On these two pages you'll find some of our favorite dessert recipes from that book. With recipes as familiar to us today as Apple Pie, and as old-fashioned as Currant Catsup, the Gold Medal book gives us a peek into our American culinary heritage. Perhaps what's most fun about looking through those yellowed pages is learning that while cooking directions may have changed dramatically, many recipes are fundamentally the same. The old ones often sound funny—but we can be sure that they were just as delicious as the recipes we use today! Compare the Mince Pie here to Apricot-Mince Pie (page 46), and the Ginger Snaps with today's Gingersnaps (page 102). Enjoy a bit of Betty Crocker heritage with us in this section, but be sure to use the up-to-date recipes in the chapters that follow. The current recipes have all the charm and flavor of the old ones . . . and we think you'll find them a lot easier to use!

Cherry Tart

◇◇◇◇◇◇◇

Line a deep pie dish with plain paste. Pick over 1 1/2 pounds of cherries; turn a tiny cup upside down in the middle, fill around it with the fruit, add sugar to taste. Lay a wide strip of plain paste around the edge of the dish, cover and press the edges firmly together with a pastry jagger, bake in hot oven and serve with powdered sugar sprinkled thickly on top. All juicy fruits are most excellent cooked in the same way.

Charlotte Russe, No. 1

◇◇◇◇◇◇◇

2 CUPS CREAM	1/2 DOZEN LADY FINGERS
1/2 CUP POWDERED SUGAR	1 TEASPOON VANILLA
1 SPECK SALT	

Mix the cream, vanilla and sugar. Set into ice water and when chilled whip to a thick froth. Drain and fling into a dish that has been lined with the cake. Keep on ice until wanted. Serve in the same dish.

Mince Pie, Plain

❖❖❖❖❖❖

TWO cups chopped beef, 4 cups sugar, 1 nutmeg, 2 cups boiled cider, 2 lemons, rind and juice, or a sour orange, 4 teaspoons salt, 4 teaspoons cinnamon, 4 cups of chopped fruit (raisins, citron, currants), 1 teaspoon cloves, 1 cup suet, finely chopped. Mix and scald, pack down in jars and pour a little brandy on top. When used add 6 cups chopped apple and stoned raisins, *ad lib*.

Ginger Snaps

❖❖❖❖❖❖

1 CUP MOLASSES	1 TABLESPOON GINGER
1 TEASPOON SODA	GOLD MEDAL FLOUR TO
1/2 CUP SUGAR	ROLL VERY THIN
1/2 CUP BUTTER	

MIX molasses, sugar, ginger and butter, stir over the fire until the butter is melted, then stir in quickly 3 cups of Gold Medal flour in which has been sifted the pulverized soda. Knead the dough until it becomes smooth and set on ice, over night if possible. Roll as thin as pasteboard and bake in a quick oven.

Brambles

❖❖❖❖❖❖

ONE lemon grated whole, 1 cup raisins, seeded and chopped fine, 1/2 cup sugar, 1 egg, 1 tablespoon cracker dust, bake in "turnovers" or patty pans, or better still, roll trimmings of puff paste as thin as possible, put a layer on a baking sheet, spread with above mixture and cover with another flat of paste. Mark off with a pastry jagger in strips four inches long by two inches wide and bake in a quick oven. These are nice with a thin icing and are delicious with cocoa for lunch. Another richer filling is made by chopping very fine 1/4 pound figs, 2 ounces citron, 1/4 cup pistachio nuts (or almonds), 2 ounces seeded raisins, add 1 egg well beaten and use like the above.

Devonshire Cream

❖❖❖❖❖❖

LET the milk stand twenty-four hours in winter (twelve in summer), then set it on the stove till almost at the boiling point. It must not bubble, but should show wrinkles and look thick. The more slowly it is done the firmer it will be. On the following day skim it by folding over and over in small rolls, and set them on ice till wanted. This is also known as "clotted cream."

Custard Pie

❖❖❖❖❖❖

2 CUPS MILK	1/4 TEASPOON SALT
1 TEASPOON GOLD MEDAL FLOUR	3 EGGS
1/2 CUP SUGAR	1/2 TEASPOON FLAVORING EXTRACT

LINE a deep pie plate with plain paste. Rub the flour smooth with 1/2 cup cold milk, add to the remainder of the milk scalded; cook five minutes. Beat the eggs and combine with sugar and salt. Pour the milk mixture over this slowly, add flavoring, strain into the plate. Bake slowly. It is done when the knife blade makes a clean cut.

CHAPTER ONE

Sweet Cobblers, Crisps and Fruit

There is something especially cozy and simple—and downright American—about a fruit dessert. A warm cobbler topped with freshly whipped cream is a pleasure we associate with casual summer meals, family gatherings and traditional Sunday suppers. Whether you start with the crunchy, tart apples of autumn's harvest or the luscious, sweet peaches of summer, your fruit dessert will have all the flavor, charm and fragrance of days gone by.

Today you can buy many kinds of fruit all year-'round, and what isn't available fresh you will probably be able to find frozen. While it's certainly nice to have the luxury of buying fruit during any season, keep in mind that fruit in season is generally less expensive. You might also find that fruit is fresher and tastier when it's in season because chances are it has been grown locally, and comes to you at the peak of its season. A blueberry crisp made from berries you picked yourself is one of the great, simple pleasures in life.

Enjoy these old-time favorites unadorned or serve them with ice cream, whipped cream or simply good, rich cream. For a pretty presentation, top the desserts with a few fresh berries or slices of fruit. To keep sliced apples, pears, peaches and bananas looking fresh, dip them immediately in lemon juice and arrange them just before serving the dessert.

Strawberry Cream Tumble (page 14), Fresh Peach-
Blueberry Cobbler (page 2)

Fresh Plum Cobbler

¾ cup sugar

3 tablespoons cornstarch

½ teaspoon ground cinnamon

2 cups unpeeled red plum slices
   (6 to 8 large)

2 cups unpeeled purple plum slices
   (6 to 8 large)

1 teaspoon lemon juice

1 cup all-purpose flour

1 tablespoon sugar

1½ teaspoons baking powder

½ teaspoon salt

3 tablespoons shortening

½ cup milk

Whipping (heavy) cream

Heat oven to 400°. Blend ¾ cup sugar, the cornstarch and cinnamon in 1½-quart saucepan. Stir in plums and lemon juice. Cook, stirring constantly, until mixture thickens and boils. Boil and stir 1 minute. Pour mixture into ungreased 2-quart casserole.

Stir together flour, 1 tablespoon sugar, the baking powder and salt. Cut in shortening thoroughly. Mix in milk. Drop mixture by 6 to 8 spoonfuls onto hot plums. Bake 25 to 30 minutes or until topping is golden brown. Serve warm with whipping cream. **6 to 8 servings.**

Fresh Peach-Blueberry Cobbler

3 cups unpeeled fresh peach slices
   (4 or 5 medium)*

1 cup fresh blueberries**

⅔ cup sugar

3 tablespoons all-purpose flour

½ teaspoon ground cinnamon

2 tablespoons butter or margarine

1 cup all-purpose flour

2 tablespoons sugar

1½ teaspoons baking powder

½ teaspoon salt

⅓ cup shortening

3 tablespoons milk

1 egg

Heat oven to 375°. Place fruits in ungreased square baking dish, 8 × 8 × 2 inches. Mix ⅔ cup sugar, 3 tablespoons flour and the cinnamon. Sprinkle over fruit. Dot with butter.

Stir together 1 cup flour, 2 tablespoons sugar, the baking powder and salt. Cut in shortening thoroughly. Mix in milk and egg. Drop mixture by 8 spoonfuls onto fruit. Bake 25 to 30 minutes or until topping is golden brown. Serve warm and, if desired, with whipping cream or ice cream. **8 servings.**

3 cups frozen sliced peaches, partially thawed and drained, can be substituted for the 3 cups fresh peach slices.

**1 cup frozen blueberries, partially thawed and drained, can be substituted for the 1 cup fresh blueberries.*

Cherry Cobbler

1¼ cups sugar
3 tablespoons cornstarch
4 cups pitted red tart cherries
¼ teaspoon almond extract
3 tablespoons shortening
1 cup all-purpose flour
1 tablespoon sugar
1½ teaspoons baking powder
½ teaspoon salt
½ cup milk

Heat oven to 400°. Mix 1¼ cups sugar and the cornstarch in 2-quart saucepan. Stir in cherries and almond extract. Cook over medium heat, stirring constantly, until mixture thickens and boils. Boil and stir 1 minute. Pour into ungreased 2-quart casserole.

Stir together flour, 1 tablespoon sugar, the baking powder and salt. Cut in shortening thoroughly. Mix in milk. Drop dough by 6 to 8 spoonfuls onto hot cherry mixture. Bake 25 to 30 minutes or until topping is golden brown. Serve warm with whipping (heavy) cream if desired. **6 to 8 servings.**

Apple-Apricot Crisp

4 medium tart cooking apples, pared and sliced
1 cup chopped dried apricots (about 6 ounces)
¾ cup all-purpose flour
¾ cup packed brown sugar
⅓ cup chopped nuts
3 tablespoons butter or margarine, softened
Whipping (heavy) cream or ice cream

Heat oven to 350°. Place apples in ungreased square pan, 8 × 8 × 2 inches. Top with apricots. Mix remaining ingredients, except whipping cream; sprinkle over apples and apricots. Bake 35 to 40 minutes or until apples are tender. Serve warm with whipping cream. **9 servings.**

Note: If apricots are very dry, cover with boiling water and let stand 3 minutes; drain.

Before the introduction of trains with refrigerated compartments, only locally grown produce was available to most Americans. Therefore, different areas of the country had fruit desserts particular to that region. Cherry cobblers were a midwestern mainstay, for example, while cranberries, apples and blueberries were used in the Northeast, and peaches graced cobblers of the South.

Blueberry-Pineapple Buckle

*1 can (8¼ ounces) crushed pineapple in
  syrup*
1¼ cups all-purpose flour
½ cup sugar
¼ cup butter or margarine, softened
¼ cup shortening
½ cup milk
1½ teaspoons baking powder
1 teaspoon grated lemon peel, if desired
½ teaspoon vanilla
¼ teaspoon salt
1 egg
1 cup fresh blueberries*
Crumb Topping (below)
Pineapple Sauce (right)

Heat oven to 350°. Drain pineapple, reserving
syrup for Pineapple Sauce. Mix flour, sugar, butter, shortening, milk, baking powder, lemon peel,
vanilla, salt and egg. Fold in blueberries and
pineapple. Spread in ungreased square pan,
8 × 8 × 2 inches. Prepare Crumb Topping.
Sprinkle over batter. Bake 45 to 50 minutes or
until golden brown and toothpick inserted in
center comes out clean. Serve warm with Pineapple Sauce. **9 servings.**

**1 cup frozen blueberries, thawed and well drained,
can be substituted for the fresh blueberries.*

Crumb Topping

½ cup sugar
⅓ cup all-purpose flour
¼ cup butter or margarine, softened
½ teaspoon ground cinnamon

Mix all ingredients until crumbly.

Pineapple Sauce

2 tablespoons packed brown sugar
1 teaspoon cornstarch
Reserved pineapple syrup
¼ teaspoon lemon juice

Mix brown sugar and cornstarch in 1-quart saucepan. Add enough water to pineapple syrup to
measure ⅔ cup; stir into brown sugar mixture.
Cook over medium heat, stirring constantly, until mixture boils. Boil and stir 1 minute; remove
from heat. Stir in lemon juice. Serve warm.

Blueberry Crisp

3 cups fresh blueberries*
2 tablespoons lemon juice
⅔ cup packed brown sugar
½ cup all-purpose flour
½ cup regular or quick-cooking oats
⅓ cup butter or margarine, softened
¼ teaspoon salt
¾ teaspoon ground cinnamon
Whipping (heavy) cream or ice cream

Heat oven to 375°. Place blueberries in ungreased square baking pan, 8 × 8 × 2 inches.
Sprinkle with lemon juice. Mix remaining ingredients, except whipping cream until crumbly;
sprinkle over blueberries. Bake about 30 minutes or until topping is golden brown. Serve
warm with whipping cream. **6 servings.**

**1 package (16 ounces) frozen blueberries can be
substituted for the 3 cups fresh blueberries; do not
thaw.*

Blueberry Crisp, Blueberry-Pineapple Buckle

Apple~Blackberry Pandowdy

Halfway through baking, the topping is cut into the fruit filling, making a wonderfully homey dessert.

4 medium tart cooking apples, pared and thinly sliced (about 4 cups)
2 cups fresh blackberries*
½ cup sugar
½ teaspoon ground cinnamon
¼ teaspoon salt
¼ teaspoon ground nutmeg
⅓ cup maple syrup or light molasses
2 tablespoons butter or margarine, melted
Pastry (right)
2 tablespoons butter or margarine, melted
Whipping (heavy) cream or sweetened whipped cream

Heat oven to 350°. Mix apples, blackberries, sugar, cinnamon, salt and nutmeg. Turn into ungreased 2-quart casserole. Mix syrup and 2 tablespoons butter. Pour over fruit mixture.

Prepare Pastry. Cut slits near center; fit pastry over fruit inside rim of casserole. Brush with 3 tablespoons butter. Bake 30 minutes; remove from oven. Cut crust into small pieces with sharp knife, mixing pieces into fruit filling.

Bake about 30 minutes or until apples are tender and pieces of crust are golden. Serve warm with whipping cream. 6 servings.

*2 cups frozen blackberries, thawed and drained, can be substituted for the 2 cups fresh blackberries.

Pastry

1¼ cups all-purpose flour
¼ teaspoon salt
¼ cup lard or ⅓ cup shortening
3 to 4 tablespoons milk

Mix flour and salt. Cut in lard until particles are size of small peas. Sprinkle with milk, 1 tablespoon at a time, tossing with fork until all flour is moistened and pastry almost cleans side of bowl. Gather pastry into ball; shape into flattened round on lightly floured cloth-covered surface. Roll with floured cloth-covered rolling pin into shape to fit top of casserole.

DESSERTS THEN

"Cake," "pie" and "cookie" sound tame when compared to some of the wonderfully bizarre names for other old-fashioned desserts. Strangely enough, these funny names are quite practical; they actually describe the dessert. The top of a buckle, for example, has a buckled and cracked appearance. We "dowdy" a pandowdy by cutting the biscuit top into the fruit partway through baking. Cobblers can be "cobbled up," meaning they can be thrown together quickly. And, the dough of a roly-poly is rolled up jellyroll-fashion before the dessert is steamed.

Apple-Blackberry Pandowdy

Peach Dumplings with Brandy Cream

2 cups all-purpose flour
3/4 teaspoon salt
2/3 cup lard or 2/3 cup plus 2 tablespoons shortening
4 to 5 tablespoons cold water
6 peaches, peeled, halved and pitted
3 tablespoons raisins
3 tablespoons chopped nuts
2 1/2 cups packed brown sugar
1 1/3 cups water
Brandy Cream (right)

Heat oven to 400°. Mix flour and salt. Cut in lard until particles are size of small peas. Sprinkle with cold water, 1 tablespoon at a time, tossing with fork until all flour is moistened and pastry almost cleans side of bowl. Gather pastry into ball; reserve one-third of the pastry. Shape remaining pastry into flattened round on lightly floured cloth-covered surface. Roll pastry into 14-inch square; cut into 4 squares. Roll reserved pastry into rectangle, 14 × 7 inches; cut into 2 squares.

Place 1 peach half, flat side up, on each square. Mix raisins and nuts; fill center of each peach half. Top with remaining peach halves. Moisten corners of square; bring 2 opposite corners of pastry up over peach and press corners together. Fold in sides of remaining corners; bring corners up over peach and press together. Place dumplings in rectangular baking pan, 13 × 9 × 2 inches. Heat brown sugar and 1 1/3 cups water to boiling; carefully pour around dumplings. Spoon syrup over dumplings about 5 minutes before dumplings are done. Bake about 40 minutes or until crust is brown and peach is tender. Serve warm with Brandy Cream. **6 servings.**

Brandy Cream

1 egg
3/4 cup whipping (heavy) cream
1/4 cup sugar
1 tablespoon brandy or 1/2 teaspoon brandy flavoring

Beat egg in 1-quart saucepan until foamy. Heat egg, whipping cream and sugar over medium heat, stirring constantly, until mixture thickens and boils. Boil and stir 1 minute; remove from heat. Stir in brandy. Serve warm or refrigerate.

Peach Dumplings with Brandy Cream

Cherry-Coconut Brown Betty

Brown betties have graced American tables since the eighteenth century. Made of fruit and bread crumbs, they are wonderfully simple and delicious. This unusual version combines native pecans and tropical coconut with the standard fruit and pastry.

> *4 cups soft bread crumbs (about 5 slices bread)*
> *½ cup shredded coconut*
> *2 tablespoons butter or margarine, melted*
> *1¼ cups sugar*
> *2 tablespoons all-purpose flour*
> *2 pounds fresh red tart cherries, pitted (about 4½ cups)**
> *¼ cup shredded coconut*
> *¼ cup chopped pecans*
> *2 tablespoons butter or margarine, softened*

Heat oven to 350°. Mix bread crumbs, ½ cup coconut and 2 tablespoons melted butter. Mix sugar and flour; stir in cherries. Sprinkle half of the bread crumb mixture in ungreased square pan, 8 × 8 × 2 inches; top with half of the cherry mixture. Repeat with remaining bread crumb and cherry mixtures. Mix ¼ cup coconut, the pecans and 2 tablespoons softened butter; sprinkle over cherry mixture.

Bake 25 to 35 minutes or until topping is golden brown. Serve warm. **6 servings.**

*2 cans (about 16 ounces each) pitted red tart cherries, drained, can be substituted for the fresh red tart cherries.

Gingered Peach Crunch

> *1 cup crushed Gingersnaps, about 9 cookies (page 102)*
> *½ cup packed brown sugar*
> *1 teaspoon ground cinnamon*
> *½ teaspoon ground nutmeg*
> *⅓ cup firm butter or margarine*
> *4 medium fresh peaches, peeled and sliced (about 4 cups)**
> *½ cup coarsely chopped pecans*

Heat oven to 375°. Mix Gingersnap crumbs, brown sugar, cinnamon and nutmeg. Cut in butter until crumbly. Toss 1 cup of the gingersnap mixture and the peaches. Spread in ungreased square pan, 8 × 8 × 2 inches. Mix pecans and remaining gingersnap mixture; sprinkle over peaches. Bake about 25 minutes or until peaches are tender. Serve warm. **6 servings.**

*2 packages (16 ounces each) frozen sliced peaches, thawed and well drained, can be substituted for the fresh peaches.

Rhubarb Roly-Poly

2 cups cut-up rhubarb
2/3 to 1 cup sugar
2 tablespoons all-purpose flour
1¾ cups all-purpose flour
1 cup whipping (heavy) cream
2½ teaspoons baking powder
½ teaspoon salt
2 tablespoons butter or margarine, softened
Whipping (heavy) cream

Mix rhubarb, sugar and 2 tablespoons flour; reserve. Mix 1¾ cups flour, 1 cup whipping cream, the baking powder and salt with fork until dough leaves side of bowl and rounds into a ball. (If dough is too dry, mix in 1 to 2 tablespoons additional whipping cream.) Turn dough onto lightly floured surface. Knead lightly 10 times, sprinkling with flour if dough is too sticky. Roll or pat dough into rectangle, 10 × 8 inches. Spread rectangle with butter. Sprinkle reserved rhubarb mixture to within ½ inch of edges; press lightly into dough.

Roll up, beginning at wide edge. Pinch edge of dough into roll to seal well. (Moisten dough with water, if necessary, to seal.) Wrap loosely in clean towel.

Place two 6-ounce custard cups in 8-quart Dutch oven. Fill Dutch oven with water to within 1 inch of tops of cups. Place heatproof dinner plate on custard cups. Cover Dutch oven; heat water to boiling. Place loosely wrapped roll on plate in Dutch oven. Cover; reduce heat and simmer 1 hour. Carefully remove hot plate from Dutch oven. Unwrap roll; cut into slices. Serve warm with whipping cream. **6 to 8 servings.**

Raspberry-Cranberry Slump

¾ cup sugar
2 tablespoons cornstarch
½ cup water
2½ cups fresh raspberries*
1½ cups fresh cranberries**
1 cup all-purpose flour
2 tablespoons sugar
1½ teaspoons baking powder
¼ teaspoon salt
¼ teaspoon ground cinnamon
¼ cup firm butter or margarine
⅓ cup milk
Whipping (heavy) cream

Mix ¾ cup sugar and the cornstarch in 3-quart saucepan. Stir in water until well blended. Stir in raspberries and cranberries. Cook over medium heat, stirring constantly, until mixture thickens and boils. Boil and stir 1 minute.

Mix flour, 2 tablespoons sugar, the baking powder, salt and cinnamon in small bowl. Cut in butter until mixture resembles fine crumbs. Stir in milk. Drop dough by 6 spoonfuls onto hot fruit mixture.

Cook uncovered over low heat 10 minutes; cover and cook 10 minutes longer. Serve warm with whipping cream. **6 servings.**

*2½ cups frozen raspberries, thawed, can be substituted for the fresh raspberries.

**1½ cups frozen cranberries, thawed, can be substituted for the fresh cranberries.

Maple-baked Winter Pears

Bosc, Anjou and Comice are all winter pears. For baking, choose pears that yield only slightly when pressed lightly.

6 pears, pared, cut in half and cored
½ cup packed brown sugar
⅓ cup maple syrup
¼ cup water
2 teaspoons grated lemon peel
⅛ teaspoon ground ginger

Heat oven to 350°. Place pears, cut sides down, in ungreased rectangular pan, 13 × 9 × 2 inches. Mix remaining ingredients. Pour over pears. Bake uncovered 20 to 25 minutes, brushing pears occasionally with syrup, until tender. Serve warm. **6 servings.**

Strawberry-Raspberry Fool

Fools have been enjoyed in England since the sixteenth century. They are rich with ripe fruit and whipped cream, an absolutely luscious summer dessert!

1 cup sliced fresh strawberries*
1 cup fresh raspberries**
⅓ cup powdered sugar
1½ cups whipping (heavy) cream
¼ cup powdered sugar

Place strawberries, raspberries and ⅓ cup powdered sugar in blender. Cover and blend on medium speed, stopping blender frequently to stir mixture, until smooth; strain. Beat whipping cream and ¼ cup powdered sugar in chilled medium bowl until stiff. Fold in strained berry mixture. Spoon into serving dishes. Cover and refrigerate at least 2 hours or until chilled. Garnish with additional berries if desired. **4 servings.**

*1 package (10 ounces) frozen strawberries, thawed and drained, can be substituted for the fresh strawberries. Decrease ⅓ cup powdered sugar to 3 tablespoons.

**1 package (10 ounces) frozen raspberries, thawed and drained, can be substituted for the fresh raspberries. Decrease ⅓ cup powdered sugar to 3 tablespoons.

Note: If using both frozen strawberries and raspberries, omit ⅓ cup powdered sugar.

Strawberry-Raspberry Fool, Rhubarb Roly-Poly (page 11)

Strawberry Cream Tumble

½ cup powdered sugar
1 quart strawberries, sliced
1 cup whipping (heavy) cream
2 tablespoons powdered sugar
3 or 4 tablespoons orange-flavored liqueur,
*   if desired*

Sprinkle ½ cup powdered sugar on strawberries; stir gently. Cover and refrigerate at least 2 hours but no longer than 24 hours.

Beat whipping cream and 2 tablespoons powdered sugar in chilled medium bowl until stiff; fold in liqueur. Fold into strawberries. Refrigerate any remaining dessert immediately. **6 servings.**

Raspberry Summer Pudding

8 to 10 thin slices firm white bread
4 cups red raspberries
⅔ cup sugar
1 teaspoon lemon juice
Whipping (heavy) cream or whipped cream

Trim crusts from bread. Arrange about three-fourths of the bread on bottom and up side of 1½-quart bowl, soufflé dish or pudding mold, cutting slices to fit shape of bowl. Heat raspberries, sugar and lemon juice over low heat about 5 minutes, gently stirring occasionally, until juice forms; cool slightly.

Spoon raspberries into bread-lined bowl, using slotted spoon. Pour juice evenly over raspberries and bread. Cover raspberries with remaining bread (use additional slices of bread if necessary to cover the top evenly). Cover with a plate that fits inside bowl, pressing plate gently onto bread. Place a weight on plate (an unopened fruit or vegetable can works well). Refrigerate at least 24 hours.

Loosen edge of pudding with thin knife or spatula. Invert into shallow serving dish. Serve with whipping cream. **8 servings.**

Layered Banana Dessert

Amber Sauce (right)
27 graham cracker squares
2 cups whipping (heavy) cream
½ teaspoon ground cinnamon
3 medium bananas

Prepare Amber Sauce. Arrange 9 square graham crackers in ungreased square baking dish, 8 × 8 × 2 inches. Beat whipping cream and cinnamon in chilled bowl until soft peaks form.

Carefully spread 1⅓ cups whipped cream mixture over graham crackers in dish. Slice 1½ bananas in single layer over whipped cream. Drizzle with 3 tablespoons of Amber Sauce. Repeat with 9 graham crackers, 1⅓ cups whipped cream mixture, 1½ bananas and the Amber Sauce. Arrange remaining 9 graham crackers on top and spread with remaining whipped cream.

Cover and refrigerate at least 8 hours or until crackers are soft. Cut into squares. Serve with additional Amber Sauce. **9 servings.**

Amber Sauce

½ cup packed brown sugar
¼ cup light corn syrup
¼ cup half-and-half
2 tablespoons butter or margarine

Mix all ingredients in 1-quart saucepan. Cook over low heat, stirring occasionally, until mixture boils. Refrigerate uncovered about 45 minutes or until cool.

Ambrosia

Mere mortals enjoy this simple orange and coconut dessert, named "Ambrosia" to recall the favorite food of the mythological Greek gods.

4 medium oranges, pared and thinly sliced
½ cup flaked coconut
2 tablespoons sugar

Layer one-fourth of the oranges, coconut and sugar in serving bowl. Repeat three times. Cover and refrigerate at least 2 hours but no longer than 24 hours. **6 servings.**

CHAPTER TWO
Classic Cakes

The first *Betty Crocker's Cookbook* in 1950 included these inspiring words about cakes: "A butter icing is like a favorite cotton dress . . . simple and easy to put on . . . cooked white frostings are like a perky street ensemble . . . and the extra touches of tinted coconut, toasted nuts or allegretti are the gay accessories that make a costume 'special.' Your family will enjoy your 'dressed-up' cakes the more because they look so pretty."

We still love to "dress up" cakes to celebrate birthday parties, weddings, even coffee hours and every occasion in between. There's something very satisfying about whipping up a regal layer cake, a classic chocolate cake or a traditional fruitcake, and something even more satisfying about eating one.

As you look through these pages, you'll notice how advances in cooking techniques and ingredients, and actual historical events too (such as the Civil War), have changed the way we bake cakes. Just think: Even in the early part of this century, preheating the oven was no simple affair. *The Washburn Crosby Gold Medal Flour Cook Book* recommended the following method for testing the oven temperature: "If a piece of white paper turns a deep yellow in five minutes the oven is ready for butter cakes; if it turns a light yellow in five minutes it is ready for sponge cake."

The twentieth century also saw the invention of new kinds of cake. The centuries-old sponge cake, leavened only with stiffly beaten eggs, has now been joined by such innovative specialties as chiffon cakes, invented by a traveling salesman in 1927 and popularized by Betty Crocker in 1948.

Eggnog Pound Cake (page 20), Chocolate Buttermallow Cake (page 18)

Chocolate Buttermallow Cake

1³/₄ cups all-purpose flour or cake flour
1 cup granulated sugar
¹/₂ cup packed brown sugar
1¹/₂ teaspoons baking soda
³/₄ teaspoon salt
1¹/₄ cups buttermilk
¹/₂ cup shortening
2 eggs
1 teaspoon vanilla
¹/₂ teaspoon red food color
2 ounces unsweetened chocolate, melted and cooled, or 1 bar (4 ounces) sweet cooking chocolate, melted and cooled
Butterscotch Filling (right)
¹/₂ cup chopped nuts
Marshmallow Frosting (right)
¹/₂ ounce unsweetened chocolate

Heat oven to 350°. Grease and flour 2 round pans, 9 × 1¹/₂ inches. Beat flour, granulated sugar, brown sugar, baking soda, salt, buttermilk, shortening, eggs and vanilla in large bowl on low speed 45 seconds, scraping bowl constantly. Beat in food color and 2 ounces chocolate on high speed 3 minutes, scraping bowl occasionally. Pour into pans.

Bake 25 to 30 minutes or until toothpick inserted in center comes out clean. Cool 10 minutes; remove from pans and cool completely. Prepare Butterscotch Filling. Fill layers to within ¹/₂ inch of edge; sprinkle with half of the nuts. Spread remaining filling on top of cake to within ¹/₂ inch of edge; sprinkle with remaining nuts. Prepare Marshmallow Frosting. Frost sides and top of cake with frosting. Heat ¹/₂ ounce chocolate over low heat until melted. Dip back of spoon into chocolate and form swirls on frosting. **16 servings.**

Butterscotch Filling

¹/₂ cup packed light brown sugar
¹/₄ cup cornstarch
¹/₄ teaspoon salt
¹/₂ cup water
1 tablespoon butter or margarine

Mix brown sugar, cornstarch and salt in 1-quart saucepan. Stir in water. Cook, stirring constantly, until mixture thickens and boils. Boil and stir 1 minute. Stir in butter; cool.

Marshmallow Frosting

2 egg whites
1¹/₂ cups sugar
¹/₄ teaspoon cream of tartar
1 tablespoon light corn syrup
¹/₃ cup water
³/₄ cup marshmallow creme

Mix egg whites, sugar, cream of tartar, corn syrup and water in top of double boiler. Place over boiling water. Beat with hand beater until stiff peaks form, scraping pan occasionally; remove from heat. Add marshmallow creme and continue beating until frosting is of spreading consistency.

Hazelnut Chocolate Torte

6 eggs, separated
1 tablespoon finely shredded orange peel
¾ teaspoon ground cinnamon
½ cup granulated sugar
1 teaspoon cream of tartar
½ cup granulated sugar
3 cups very finely ground hazelnuts
½ cup all-purpose flour
Chocolate Butter Frosting (right)
1 cup whipping (heavy) cream
½ cup powdered sugar
¼ cup cocoa
2 teaspoons finely shredded orange peel
½ cup finely chopped hazelnuts

Heat oven to 325°. Grease bottom only of springform pan, 9 × 3 inches. Line bottom with waxed paper; grease generously. Beat egg yolks, 1 tablespoon orange peel and the cinnamon in medium bowl on high speed about 6 minutes or until very thick and lemon colored. Gradually beat in ½ cup sugar, 1 tablespoon at a time; reserve. Wash beaters.

Beat egg whites and cream of tartar in large bowl on high speed until soft peaks form. Gradually beat in ½ cup sugar, 1 tablespoon at a time. Continue beating until stiff peaks form. Fold egg yolk mixture into egg white mixture. Mix 3 cups ground hazelnuts and the flour. Sprinkle about one-third of the hazelnut mixture over egg mixture; fold in. Repeat with remaining hazelnut mixture. Spread in pan.

Bake 55 to 60 minutes or until toothpick inserted in center comes out clean. Cool 15 minutes; loosen side of cake from pan. Carefully remove side of pan. Invert cake onto wire rack; remove bottom of pan. Turn cake right side up and cool completely. Wrap tightly; refrigerate at least 4 hours.

Carefully split cake horizontally to make 3 layers (To split, mark side of cake with toothpicks and cut with long, thin serrated knife.)

Prepare Chocolate Butter Frosting. Reserve 1 cup for decorating. Beat whipping cream, powdered sugar and cocoa in chilled small bowl until stiff. Fold in 2 teaspoons orange peel. Spread 1 cake layer with half of the whipped cream mixture; repeat. Top with remaining cake layer.

Frost side and top of torte with Chocolate Butter Frosting. Press ½ cup chopped hazelnuts around side.

Place reserved 1 cup Chocolate Butter Frosting in decorating bag with large open star tip. Pipe rosettes on top of cake. Garnish with whole hazelnuts if desired. Refrigerate at least 8 hours. To cut, use sharp, straight-edge knife. Refrigerate any remaining torte. **16 servings.**

Chocolate Butter Frosting

½ cup butter or margarine, softened
3 ounces unsweetened chocolate, melted and
*   cooled, or ½ cup cocoa*
3 cups powdered sugar
1 tablespoon brandy, if desired
2 teaspoons vanilla
About 3 tablespoons milk

Mix butter and chocolate in medium bowl. Beat in remaining ingredients until mixture is smooth and of spreading consistency.

Chocolate-Pecan Bourbon Cake

2 cups all-purpose flour or cake flour
2 cups granulated sugar
½ cup butter or margarine, softened
¾ cup buttermilk
½ cup water
¼ cup bourbon
1 teaspoon baking soda
1 teaspoon vanilla
½ teaspoon salt
½ teaspoon baking powder
2 eggs
4 ounces unsweetened chocolate, melted and cooled
1 cup chopped pecans
Powdered sugar

Heat oven to 350°. Grease and flour tube pan, 10 × 4 inches, or 12-cup bundt cake pan. Beat all ingredients except pecans and powdered sugar in large bowl on low speed 30 seconds, scraping bowl constantly. Beat on high speed 3 minutes, scraping bowl occasionally. Stir in pecans. Pour into pan.

Bake 60 to 65 minutes or until toothpick inserted in center comes out clean. Cool 10 minutes; remove from pan. Turn rounded side up and cool completely. Dust with powdered sugar. **16 servings.**

Eggnog Pound Cake

1 cup sugar
½ cup butter or margarine, softened
2 tablespoons rum or 2 teaspoons rum flavoring
1 teaspoon vanilla
5 egg yolks
1¾ cups all-purpose flour
2 teaspoons baking powder
¾ teaspoon salt
½ teaspoon ground nutmeg
¾ cup milk

Heat oven to 350°. Grease and flour loaf pan, 9 × 5 × 3 inches. Beat sugar, butter, rum, vanilla and egg yolks in large bowl on low speed 30 seconds, scraping bowl constantly. Beat on high speed 5 minutes, scraping bowl occasionally. Beat in flour, baking powder, salt and nutmeg alternately with milk on low speed. Pour into pan.

Bake 50 to 60 minutes or until toothpick inserted in center comes out clean. Cool 10 minutes; remove from pan and cool completely. **16 servings.**

Lazy Daisy Cake

This is the perfect cake for a "lazy" baker— or for one who wants to make a cake in a hurry. Broiling the easy frosting right on the top of the cake has been a popular technique since the 1930s. Your guests will never imagine that the delicious, bubbling, golden brown frosting is a shortcut!

>   *1½ cups cake flour or 1¼ cups all-purpose*
>   *flour*
>   *1 cup sugar*
>   *¾ cup milk*
>   *⅓ cup butter or margarine, softened*
>   *1½ teaspoons baking powder*
>   *1 teaspoon vanilla*
>   *½ teaspoon salt*
>   *1 egg*
>   *Broiled Coconut Frosting (right)*

Heat oven to 350°. Grease and flour square pan, 8 × 8 × 2 or 9 × 9 × 2 inches. Beat all ingredients except Broiled Coconut Frosting on low speed 30 seconds, scraping bowl constantly. Beat on high speed 3 minutes, scraping bowl occasionally. Pour into pan. Bake 35 to 40 minutes or until toothpick inserted in center comes out clean.

Set oven control to broil. Prepare Broiled Coconut Frosting; spread over hot cake. Broil with top of cake about 4 inches from heat about 2 minutes or until frosting is light brown. Serve warm. **9 servings.**

Broiled Coconut Frosting

>   *1 cup flaked coconut*
>   *⅓ cup packed brown sugar*
>   *¼ cup butter or margarine, softened*
>   *2 tablespoons half-and-half*

Mix all ingredients.

Peanut Butter Cake

Peanut butter is appreciated nowhere else like it is in America. Invented at the end of the last century, it was originally developed as a healthy food for older people. While peanut butter is still loved by every age group, we think this cake will be especially popular with the lunch-box crowd.

>   *1½ cups all-purpose flour*
>   *¾ cup sugar*
>   *⅓ cup peanut butter*
>   *¼ cup butter or margarine, softened*
>   *¾ cup milk*
>   *2 teaspoons baking powder*
>   *¼ teaspoon salt*
>   *2 eggs*
>   *¼ cup peanut butter chips*
>   *¼ cup semisweet chocolate chips*

Heat oven to 350°. Grease and flour round pan, 9 × 1½ inches, or square pan, 8 × 8 × 2 inches. Beat all ingredients except peanut butter chips and chocolate chips on low speed 30 seconds, scraping bowl constantly. Beat on high speed 3 minutes, scraping bowl occasionally. Pour into pan. Sprinkle with chips.

Bake 35 to 40 minutes or until toothpick inserted in center comes out clean; cool. **8 servings.**

One-Egg Cake

2 cups cake flour or 1¾ cups plus 2 table-
  spoons all-purpose flour
1¼ cups sugar
2½ teaspoons baking powder
¾ teaspoon salt
⅓ cup shortening
1 teaspoon vanilla
1 cup milk
1 egg
Vanilla Silk Frosting (below)

Heat oven to 350°. Grease and flour 2 round pans, 8 × 1½ inches. Mix flour, sugar, baking powder and salt in large bowl. Add shortening, vanilla and ⅔ cup of the milk. Beat on low speed 30 seconds, scraping bowl constantly. Beat on medium speed 2 minutes, scraping bowl occasionally. Add remaining milk and the egg. Beat on medium speed 2 minutes, scraping bowl frequently. Pour into pans. Bake 25 to 30 minutes or until toothpick inserted in center comes out clean. Cool 10 minutes; remove from pans and cool completely. Fill layers with walnut mixture. Frost side and top of cake with remaining frosting. **16 servings.**

Vanilla Silk Frosting

3 cups powdered sugar
¾ cup butter or margarine, softened
1 teaspoon vanilla
3 tablespoons milk
½ cup chopped walnuts, pecans or hazel-
  nuts, toasted

Beat powdered sugar, butter and vanilla in medium bowl on low speed until blended. Gradually beat in milk on medium speed until smooth and fluffy. Mix ¾ cup of the frosting and the walnuts.

Washington Pie

1½ cups cake flour or 1¼ cups all-purpose
  flour
1 cup granulated sugar
⅓ cup shortening
¾ cup milk
1½ teaspoons baking powder
1 teaspoon vanilla
½ teaspoon salt
1 egg
¾ cup raspberry jelly
Powdered sugar

Heat oven to 350°. Grease and flour round pan, 9 × 1½ inches. Beat all ingredients except raspberry jelly and powdered sugar on low speed 30 seconds, scraping bowl constantly. Beat on high speed 3 minutes, scraping bowl occasionally. Pour into pan.

Bake about 35 minutes or until toothpick inserted in center comes out clean; cool. Split cake horizontally into halves. Fill layers with raspberry jelly. Sprinkle top with powdered sugar. **8 servings.**

Lady Baltimore Cake

Mrs. Mayberry, one of the characters in the turn-of-the century novel *Lady Baltimore*, created this perennially popular southern cake. The dried fruits and nuts mixed into the filling and icing look wonderful against the pure white cake. This cake is snowy white because no egg yolks are used and vegetable shortening is used instead of butter.

2¼ cups all-purpose flour
1⅔ cups sugar
3½ teaspoons baking powder
¾ teaspoon salt
1¼ cups milk
⅔ cup shortening
1 teaspoon vanilla
5 egg whites
½ cup raisins, chopped
6 dried figs, cut up
3 tablespoons cognac or brandy or
  1 tablespoon brandy flavoring
½ cup chopped pecans
Seven-Minute Frosting (right)

Heat oven to 350°. Grease and flour 2 round pans, 9 × 1½ inches. Beat flour, sugar, baking powder, salt, milk, shortening and vanilla in large bowl on low speed 30 seconds, scraping bowl constantly. Beat on high speed 2 minutes, scraping bowl occasionally. Beat in egg whites on high speed 2 minutes, scraping bowl occasionally. Pour into pans.

Bake 30 to 35 minutes or until toothpick inserted in center comes out clean. Cool 10 minutes; remove from pans and cool completely.

Mix raisins, figs and cognac. Let stand about 1 hour or until cognac is absorbed. Stir in pecans. Prepare Seven-Minute Frosting. Stir raisin mixture into 1 cup of the frosting; fill layers. Frost cake with remaining frosting. **16 servings.**

Seven-Minute Frosting

1½ cups sugar
¼ teaspoon cream of tartar or 1 table-
  spoon light corn syrup
⅓ cup water
2 egg whites
1 teaspoon vanilla

Mix sugar, cream of tartar, water and egg whites in top of double boiler. Beat on high speed 1 minute. Place over boiling water (water should not touch bottom of pan). Beat on high speed 7 minutes. Remove pan from water; add vanilla. Beat on high speed 2 minutes.

Lady Baltimore Cake, Lord Baltimore Cake (page 26)

Lord Baltimore Cake

Legend has it that this cake was named for one Lord Baltimore, an early English settler. It is a lovely yellow cake with a festive pink frosting.

2¼ cups all-purpose flour
1½ cups sugar
3½ teaspoons baking powder
1 teaspoon salt
1¼ cups milk
3 eggs
½ cup shortening
1 teaspoon vanilla
Pink Mountain Frosting (right)
½ cup flaked coconut, toasted
¼ cup chopped pecans or blanched almonds, toasted
¼ cup chopped maraschino cherries

Heat oven to 350°. Grease and flour 2 round pans, 9 × 1½ inches. Beat flour, sugar, baking powder, salt, milk, eggs, shortening and vanilla on low speed 30 seconds, scraping bowl constantly. Beat on high speed 3 minutes, scraping bowl occasionally. Pour into pans.

Bake 30 to 35 minutes or until toothpick inserted in center comes out clean or until cake springs back when touched lightly in center. Cool 10 minutes; remove from pans and cool completely.

Prepare Pink Mountain Frosting. Stir coconut, pecans and cherries into 1 cup of the frosting. Fill layers with half of the coconut mixture; spread remainder over top of cake. Frost side and top of cake with remaining frosting. **16 servings.**

Pink Mountain Frosting

½ cup sugar
¼ cup light corn syrup
2 tablespoons maraschino cherry syrup
2 egg whites
1 teaspoon vanilla

Mix sugar, corn syrup and maraschino cherry syrup in 1-quart saucepan. Cover and heat to rolling boil over medium heat. Uncover and boil rapidly to 242° on candy thermometer or until small amount of mixture dropped into very cold water forms a ball that flattens when removed from water.

Meanwhile, beat egg whites in medium bowl until stiff peaks form. Pour hot syrup very slowly in a thin stream into egg whites, beating constantly on medium speed. Beat on high speed until stiff peaks form. Add vanilla during last minute of beating.

Note: To toast nuts, sprinkle nuts in ungreased heavy skillet. Cook over medium heat 5 to 7 minutes, stirring frequently until nuts begin to brown, then stirring constantly until golden brown.

Note: To toast coconut, sprinkle coconut in ungreased heavy skillet. Cook over medium-low heat 6 to 14 minutes, stirring frequently until coconut begins to brown, then stirring constantly until golden brown.

Lemon-filled Poppy Seed Cake

½ cup poppy seed
1 cup milk
Lemon Filling (right)
2¼ cups cake flour or 2 cups plus 2 tablespoons all-purpose flour
1½ cups sugar
3½ teaspoons baking powder
1 teaspoon salt
½ cup shortening
1½ teaspoons vanilla
4 egg whites
Powdered sugar

Mix poppy seed and milk; let stand 1 hour. Prepare Lemon Filling.

Heat oven to 350°. Grease and flour 2 round pans 8 × 1½ or 9 × 1½ inches. Mix flour, sugar, baking powder and salt in large bowl. Add shortening, about three-fourths of the milk mixture and the vanilla. Beat on medium speed 2 minutes, scraping bowl occasionally. Beat in remaining milk mixture and the egg whites on medium speed, scraping bowl frequently. Pour into pans. Bake 30 to 35 minutes or until toothpick inserted in center comes out clean. Cool 10 minutes; remove from pans and cool completely. Fill layers with Lemon Filling. Sprinkle top of cake with powdered sugar. **16 servings.**

Lemon Filling

¾ cup sugar
3 tablespoons cornstarch
¼ teaspoon salt
¾ cup water
1 teaspoon grated lemon peel
1 tablespoon butter or margarine
⅓ cup lemon juice
4 drops yellow food color, if desired

Mix sugar, cornstarch and salt in 1-quart saucepan. Gradually stir in water. Cook over medium heat, stirring constantly, until mixture thickens and boils. Boil and stir 5 minutes. Remove from heat; stir in lemon peel and butter. Gradually stir in lemon juice and food color. Cool completely. If filling is too soft to spread, refrigerate until set.

Scripture Cake

In colonial times, people were expected to know the Bible very well. Originally, this recipe gave measurements for ingredients that were unnamed—the cook was referred to the appropriate section of the Bible to find out what was actually being measured! We'll make it easy and give you the measurements, the ingredients *and* the biblical reference.

1⅓ cups all-purpose flour	*Judges 6:19*
½ cup chopped dates	*Song of Solomon 7:7*
¼ cup butter or margarine, softened	*Genesis 18:8*
⅔ cup honey	*Genesis 43:11*
⅓ cup milk	*Isaiah 7:22*
1 teaspoon baking powder	*Leviticus 23:17 (leavening)*
½ teaspoon salt	*Ezra 6:9*
½ teaspoon ground cinnamon	*II Chronicles 9:9*
⅛ teaspoon baking soda	*Leviticus 23:17 (leavening)*
1 egg	*Deuteronomy 22:6*
Powdered sugar	*Isaiah 43:24*

Heat oven to 350°. Grease and flour square pan, 8 × 8 × 2 inches. Beat all ingredients except powdered sugar on low speed 30 seconds, scraping bowl constantly. Beat on high speed 1 minute, scraping bowl occasionally. Pour into pan. Bake 30 to 35 minutes or until toothpick inserted in center comes out clean. Cool 10 minutes; sprinkle with powdered sugar. Serve warm or cool. **9 servings.**

Apple-Cranberry Upside-down Cake

⅓ cup butter or margarine
½ cup packed brown sugar
2 medium cooking apples, pared and sliced
½ cup whole berry cranberry sauce
1⅓ cups all-purpose flour
1 cup granulated sugar
2 teaspoons baking powder
½ teaspoon salt
⅓ cup shortening
⅔ cup milk
1 teaspoon vanilla
1 egg

Heat oven to 350°. Heat butter in heavy 10-inch ovenproof skillet or square pan, 9 × 9 × 2 inches, until melted. Sprinkle brown sugar evenly over butter. Arrange apple slices in 3 rows in skillet. Spoon cranberry sauce between rows.

Mix flour, granulated sugar, baking powder and salt in large bowl. Add shortening, milk and vanilla. Beat on medium speed 2 minutes, scraping bowl constantly. Add egg. Beat on medium speed 2 minutes, scraping bowl frequently. Pour over fruit in pan.

Bake 50 minutes or until toothpick inserted in center of cake comes out clean. Immediately invert pan onto heatproof serving plate. Leave pan over cake a few minutes (brown sugar mixture will run down over cake); remove pan. Serve warm with whipped cream or ice cream if desired. **9 servings.**

Orange-Coconut Cake

2 cups all-purpose flour
1½ cups sugar
1 cup flaked coconut
¼ cup butter or margarine, softened
¼ cup shortening
1 cup milk
3½ teaspoons baking powder
1 tablespoon finely shredded orange peel
1 teaspoon salt
1 teaspoon vanilla
3 eggs
Orange Fluffy Frosting (below)

Heat oven to 350°. Grease and flour 2 round pans, 9 × 1½ inches. Beat all ingredients except Orange Fluffy Frosting on medium speed 30 seconds, scraping bowl constantly. Beat on high speed 3 minutes, scraping bowl occasionally. Pour into pans.

Bake 30 to 35 minutes or until toothpick inserted in center comes out clean. Cool 10 minutes; remove from pans and cool completely. Fill layers and frost cake with Orange Fluffy Frosting. **16 servings.**

Orange Fluffy Frosting

½ cup sugar
¼ cup light corn syrup
2 tablespoons water
2 egg whites
1 teaspoon finely shredded orange peel
4 drops yellow food color
1 or 2 drops red food color

Mix sugar, corn syrup and water in 1-quart saucepan. Cover and heat to rolling boil over medium heat. Uncover and boil rapidly to 242° on candy thermometer or until small amount of mixture dropped into very cold water forms a ball that flattens when removed from water.

As mixture boils, beat egg whites in small bowl just until stiff peaks form. Pour hot syrup very slowly in thin stream into egg whites, beating constantly on medium speed. Beat on high speed until stiff. Fold in orange peel and food colors.

Jeweled Fruitcake

2 cups dried apricots (8 ounces)
2 cups pitted dates (8 ounces)
1½ cups Brazil nuts (12 ounces)
1 cup cut-up red and green candied pineapple (⅓ pound)
1 cup drained red and green maraschino cherries
¾ cup all-purpose flour
¾ cup sugar
½ teaspoon baking powder
½ teaspoon salt
1½ teaspoons vanilla
3 eggs

Heat oven to 300°. Line loaf pan, 9 × 5 × 3 or 8½ × 4½ × 2½ inches, with aluminum foil; grease. Mix all ingredients. Spread evenly in pan. Bake 1¾ hours or until toothpick inserted in center comes out clean. If necessary, cover with foil during last 30 minutes of baking to prevent excessive browning. Remove from pan; cool. Wrap in plastic wrap or foil; store in refrigerator. **16 servings.**

Apple-Nut Cake with Velvet Rum Sauce

1 cup all-purpose flour
1 cup sugar
¼ cup shortening
1 teaspoon baking soda
½ teaspoon salt
½ teaspoon ground nutmeg
2 tablespoons water
1 egg
2 cups chopped pared cooking apples (about 2 medium)
½ cup chopped nuts
Velvet Rum Sauce (below)

Heat oven to 350°. Grease pie plate, 9 × 1¼ inches, or square pan, 8 × 8 × 2 inches. Beat all ingredients except apples, nuts and Velvet Rum Sauce in large bowl on low speed 30 seconds, scraping bowl constantly. Beat on medium speed 2 minutes, scraping bowl occasionally. Fold in apples and nuts. Spread in pie plate.

Bake 40 to 45 minutes or until toothpick inserted in center comes out clean. Serve warm with Velvet Rum Sauce. **8 servings.**

Velvet Rum Sauce

1 cup sugar
½ cup half-and-half
½ cup butter or margarine
2 tablespoons rum or 1 teaspoon rum flavoring
1 teaspoon ground nutmeg

Mix all ingredients in 2-quart saucepan. Heat to boiling over medium-low heat, stirring constantly. Serve warm.

Date Cake

1⅔ cups all-purpose flour
1 cup sugar
1 cup cut-up dates
½ cup finely chopped nuts
¼ cup butter or margarine, softened
1 cup water
1 teaspoon baking soda
1 teaspoon vanilla
½ teaspoon salt
1 egg
Lemon Butter Frosting (below)

Heat oven to 350°. Grease and flour square pan, 9 × 9 × 2 inches. Beat all ingredients except Lemon Butter Frosting on low speed 30 seconds, scraping bowl constantly. Beat on high speed 3 minutes, scraping bowl occasionally. Pour into pan.

Bake 45 to 50 minutes or until toothpick inserted in center comes out clean; cool. Frost with Lemon Butter Frosting. **9 servings.**

Lemon Butter Frosting

3 tablespoons butter or margarine, softened
1½ cups powdered sugar
1 teaspoon grated lemon peel
About 1 tablespoon lemon juice

Beat butter and powdered sugar in medium bowl until fluffy. Stir in lemon peel and lemon juice. Beat until smooth and of spreading consistency.

Banana-Nut Cake

Bananas and peanut butter have been a favorite combination for as long as we can remember. The riper the bananas you use, the stronger the banana flavor will be.

2¼ cups cake flour or 2⅓ cups all-purpose flour
1⅔ cups sugar
⅔ cup finely chopped nuts
1¼ cups mashed bananas (about 3 medium)
⅔ cup shortening
⅔ cup buttermilk
1¼ teaspoons baking powder
1¼ teaspoons baking soda
¾ teaspoon salt
3 eggs
Peanut Butter Frosting (right)

Heat oven to 350°. Grease and flour rectangular pan, 13 × 9 × 2 inches, or 2 round pans, 9 × 1½ inches. Beat all ingredients except Peanut Butter Frosting on low speed 30 seconds, scraping bowl constantly. Beat on high speed 3 minutes, scraping bowl occasionally. Pour into pan(s).

Bake rectangle 45 to 50 minutes, rounds 35 to 40 minutes or until toothpick inserted in center comes out clean. Cool 10 minutes; remove from pans and cool completely. Frost with Peanut Butter Frosting. **16 servings.**

Peanut Butter Frosting

⅓ cup peanut butter
3 cups powdered sugar
1½ teaspoons vanilla
¼ to ⅓ cup milk

Mix peanut butter and powdered sugar in medium bowl. Stir in vanilla and milk. Beat until smooth and of spreading consistency.

Cinnamon Cake

1½ cups all-purpose flour
1 cup sugar
1 tablespoon ground cinnamon
¼ teaspoon salt
½ cup shortening
¾ cup sour cream
1 teaspoon baking soda
1 teaspoon baking powder
2 eggs

Heat oven to 350°. Grease and flour square pan, 9 × 9 × 2 inches. Stir together flour, sugar, cinnamon and salt in large bowl. Cut in shortening until mixture is size of small peas; reserve ⅓ cup. Beat in remaining ingredients on low speed until blended. Beat on high speed 2 minutes. Spoon into pan; spread evenly. Sprinkle reserved flour mixture over batter.

Bake 30 to 35 minutes or until toothpick inserted in center comes out clean. Serve with Apple Ice Cream (page 100), ice cream or whipped cream if desired. **9 servings.**

Banana-Nut Cake, Election Cake (page 35)

Mystery Cake

When your guests ask what your "mystery" ingredient is, you might want to remind them first that the tomato is really a fruit. This spiced cake was originally made with "put-up" tomatoes. Americans have enjoyed this version of Mystery Cake since the 1920s, when canned tomato soup was first introduced.

1½ cups all-purpose flour
1 cup sugar
½ cup raisins
½ cup chopped nuts
2 tablespoons butter or margarine, softened
1 teaspoon ground cinnamon
1 teaspoon baking soda
½ teaspoon salt
¼ teaspoon ground cloves
½ teaspoon ground nutmeg
1 egg
1 can (10¾ ounces) condensed cream of tomato soup
Browned Butter Frosting (right)

Heat oven to 325°. Grease and flour square pan, 9 × 9 × 2 inches. Beat all ingredients except Browned Butter Frosting on low speed 30 seconds, scraping bowl constantly. Beat on high speed 3 minutes, scraping bowl occasionally. Pour into pan. Bake 37 to 43 minutes or until toothpick inserted in center comes out clean. Cool completely. Frost with Browned Butter Frosting. **9 servings.**

Browned Butter Frosting

3 tablespoons butter
¾ cup powdered sugar
1 teaspoon vanilla
3 to 4 teaspoons milk

Heat butter in 1½-quart saucepan over medium heat until light brown. Beat in powdered sugar, vanilla and enough milk until of spreading consistency. If frosting becomes too stiff to spread, add more milk, ½ teaspoon at a time.

Hard Times Cake

1 cup packed brown sugar
2 teaspoons ground cinnamon
½ teaspoon ground nutmeg
½ teaspoon ground cloves
1¼ cups water
½ cup shortening
2 cups raisins
2 cups all-purpose flour
1 teaspoon baking powder
1 teaspoon baking soda
¾ teaspoon salt

Mix brown sugar, cinnamon, nutmeg, cloves, water, shortening and raisins in 3-quart saucepan. Heat to boiling, stirring constantly. Boil uncovered 3 minutes, stirring frequently; cool at least 30 minutes.

Heat oven to 325°. Grease and flour square pan, 9 × 9 × 2 inches, or loaf pan, 9 × 5 × 3 inches. Stir remaining ingredients into raisin mixture; mix thoroughly. Pour into pan.

Bake square 33 to 37 minutes, loaf 50 to 55 minutes, or until toothpick inserted in center comes out clean. (Cool loaf 10 minutes; remove from pan.) Cool square or loaf completely. **9 or 16 servings.**

Election Cake

When New Englanders gathered for election days and town meetings they brought this hearty and satisfying cake with them or bought it in town. It was the perfect bring-along for all-day events because the loaf shape makes it very portable.

1 package active dry yeast
¼ cup warm water (105° to 115°)
¾ cup lukewarm milk
¼ cup sugar
¼ teaspoon salt
2 cups all-purpose flour
½ cup butter or margarine, softened
¾ cup sugar
1 cup all-purpose flour
¾ cup raisins
½ teaspoon ground nutmeg
2 tablespoons lemon juice
1 egg

Grease loaf pan, 9 × 5 × 3 inches. Dissolve yeast in water in large bowl. Add milk, ¼ cup sugar, the salt and 2 cups flour. Beat until smooth and elastic, about 1 minute. Cover and let rise in warm place about 30 minutes or until double.

Beat butter and ¾ cup sugar until light and fluffy. Stir in 1 cup flour, raisins, nutmeg, lemon juice and egg. Stir into yeast mixture until well blended. Pour into pan; spread to level. Cover and let rise in warm place 45 minutes or until mixture is about ½ inch from top of pan.

Heat oven to 350°. Bake 45 to 55 minutes or until toothpick inserted in center comes out clean. Cool 5 minutes; remove from pan and cool completely. For best flavor, wrap and let stand 24 hours before serving. **16 servings.**

Yankee ingenuity is showcased by the many recipes that were developed to cope with food shortages. During crop failures, wars and the Depression, Americans were inspired to make delicious desserts using very limited ingredients. The Civil War, for example, saw the invention of Washington Pie, which uses split cake layers instead of lard-based crust to save on precious lard. Eggs and butter were rationed during World Wars I and II and were prohibitively expensive during the Depression. During such "hard times," One Egg Cake and Hard Times Cake were very popular—patriotic and easy on the pocket book. Betty Crocker published a cookbooklet during World War II entitled *Your Share*, and in the foreword it cautioned, "You must heed the government request to increase the use of available foods—and at the same time safeguard your family's nutrition."

Mixed Berry Shortcake

The shortcake layer here is sponge cake rather than biscuit. Before commercial baking soda and baking powder became available, beaten eggs leavened these "spongy" cakes.

3 cups sliced strawberries
3 cups raspberries
½ cup blueberries, if desired
1 cup sugar
3 eggs
¾ cup sugar
1¼ cups cake flour or 1 cup plus 2 tablespoons
*   all-purpose flour*
1½ teaspoons baking powder
½ teaspoon salt
⅓ cup hot water
1 teaspoon vanilla
½ teaspoon lemon extract
Whipping (heavy) cream or sweetened
**   whipped cream**

Mix strawberries, raspberries, blueberries and 1 cup sugar; let stand at least 1 hour.

Heat oven to 350°. Grease and flour square pan, 9 × 9 × 2 inches. Beat eggs in medium bowl on high speed until very thick and lemon colored. Gradually beat in ¾ cup sugar.

Beat in flour, baking powder and salt on low speed. Gradually beat in water, vanilla and lemon extract on low speed. Pour into pan. Bake 25 to 30 minutes or until toothpick inserted in center comes out clean. Cut warm cake into 9 pieces and cut each piece horizontally in half. Fill and top with berries. Serve with whipping cream. **9 servings.**

Angel Food Cake Deluxe

Angel food cake is thought to have originated in St. Louis, Missouri, in the midnineteenth century. Some people believe that the recipe was actually brought by slaves from the South up the Mississippi River to St. Louis. Others believe that angel food cake can be traced to the Pennsylvania Dutch.

1 cup cake flour
1½ cups powdered sugar
1½ cups egg whites (about 12)
1½ teaspoons cream of tartar
1 cup granulated sugar
1½ teaspoons vanilla
½ teaspoon almond extract
¼ teaspoon salt

Heat oven to 375°. Mix flour and powdered sugar. Beat egg whites and cream of tartar in large bowl on medium speed until foamy. Beat in granulated sugar on high speed, 2 tablespoons at a time, adding vanilla, almond extract and salt with the last addition of sugar; continue beating until meringue holds stiff peaks. Do not underbeat.

Sprinkle flour-sugar mixture, ¼ cup at a time, over meringue, folding in gently just until mixture disappears. Spread in ungreased tube pan, 10 × 4 inches. Gently cut through batter with spatula.

Bake 30 to 35 minutes or until cracks feel dry and top springs back when touched lightly. Immediately invert pan onto heatproof funnel; let hang until cake is completely cool. **16 servings.**

Mixed Berry Shortcake

Chocolate Angel Food Cake

¾ cup cake flour or ⅔ cup all-purpose flour
1½ cups powdered sugar
¼ cup cocoa
1½ cups egg whites (about 12)
1½ teaspoons cream of tartar
¼ teaspoon salt
1 cup granulated sugar
1½ teaspoons vanilla

Heat oven to 350°. Mix flour, powdered sugar and cocoa. Beat egg whites, cream of tartar and salt in large bowl until foamy. Beat in granulated sugar on high speed, 2 tablespoons at a time; continue beating until egg white mixture holds stiff peaks. Gently fold in vanilla. Sprinkle flour-sugar mixture, one-fourth at a time, over egg white mixture, folding in gently just until flour-sugar mixture disappears. Spread in ungreased tube pan, 10 × 4 inches. Gently cut through batter with spatula.

Bake 35 to 45 minutes or until top springs back when touched lightly. Immediately invert pan onto heatproof funnel; let hang until cake is completely cool. **16 servings.**

Before the development of baking soda, baking powder and cream of tartar, baking a light-textured cake was a hard job. In order to achieve a light cake, eggs were whipped laboriously, using plenty of elbow grease, sometimes for as long as a half-hour. The air beaten into the eggs made the cake light in texture as in sponge cake, a favorite for centuries. When leavening became available, angel food cake was developed in the mid-eighteenth century. It uses only the whites of eggs and cream of tartar so it is even lighter than sponge cake. Most recently, chiffon cake was invented in the twentieth century. While chiffon cake is richer than angel food cake because it uses oil and egg yolks, the egg whites and cream of tartar keep it high and light like angel food cake.

Burnt Sugar Chiffon Cake

Chiffon cake is very close to our hearts. Harry Baker, a California insurance salesman, developed this wonderfully light *and* rich cake in 1927, but would not part with his secret for more than twenty years. He decided to share the identity of his secret ingredient—vegetable oil—with Betty Crocker after listening to "Betty Crocker's Cooking School of the Air." The year 1948 saw the chiffon cake trumpeted as "the cake discovery of the century!"

1½ cups sugar
¾ cup boiling water
2 cups all-purpose flour
1½ cups sugar
1 tablespoon baking powder
¾ teaspoon salt
½ cup vegetable oil
7 egg yolks
¼ cup cold water
1 teaspoon vanilla
1 cup egg whites (7 or 8)
½ teaspoon cream of tartar
Burnt Sugar Frosting (right)

Heat 1½ cups sugar in 10-inch heavy skillet over medium-low heat until sugar begins to melt. Continue cooking, stirring occasionally, until completely melted and medium brown; remove from heat. Slowly stir in boiling water until smooth. (If any lumps remain, return to heat and melt.) Cool; reserve for cake and frosting.

Move oven rack to lowest position. Heat oven to 325°. Mix flour, 1½ cups sugar, the baking powder and salt in medium bowl.

Beat in oil, egg yolks, ½ cup of the burnt sugar mixture, the cold water and vanilla until smooth. Beat egg whites and cream of tartar in large bowl until stiff peaks form. Gradually pour egg yolk mixture over beaten whites, gently folding just until blended. Pour into ungreased tube pan, 10 × 4 inches.

Bake 60 to 65 minutes or until top springs back when touched lightly. Immediately invert pan onto heatproof funnel; let hang until cake is completely cool. Remove from pan. Frost with Burnt Sugar Frosting. **16 servings.**

Burnt Sugar Frosting

4 cups powdered sugar
½ cup butter or margarine
Reserved burnt sugar mixture
2 teaspoons vanilla
About 4 tablespoons whipping (heavy) cream

Mix powdered sugar and butter. Stir in reserved burnt sugar mixture and the vanilla. Stir in whipping cream, 1 tablespoon at a time, until of spreading consistency.

CHAPTER THREE
Our Best Pies and Tarts

Which pie really is our national favorite? Is it the apple pie that no one made quite as well as your grandmother or the cherry pie that George Washington made famous? Whatever the answer, pie is part of the American way of life. Our pies have become distinctively American, and the famed early American ingenuity can be seen in the evolution of pie baking.

Pie pans were long and deep in old England, and were called "coffins." American settlers made their pans round and shallow so as to be able to cut more servings from the pie and thus stretch their food supplies a bit further. As food became more plentiful, American pies grew to be the luscious, hearty desserts we love so much today. Early settlers were avid pie eaters, enjoying them morning, noon and night. When fruit was unavailable, pie makers substituted fillings ranging from the creamy sugar mixture in Shaker Sugar Pie (page 53) to *crackers* in Mock Apple Pie (page 56).

A slice of pie, be it the southern favorite Sweet Potato–Pecan Pie (page 52) or the heavenly Chocolate Angel Pie (page 55), is a treat that everyone enjoys. There's a pie for every taste, every holiday and every meal. Pie is truly an American institution; after all, what would Thanksgiving be without apple, pumpkin, mincemeat or pecan pie? In 1950, the Betty Crocker editors wrote, "Pie . . . a symbol of good eating in a good land."

Red Currant-glazed Grape Tart (page 57),
Sour Cream Pie (page 49)

Standard Pastry

One-Crust Pie; 9-inch

1 cup all-purpose flour
½ teaspoon salt
⅓ cup lard or ⅓ cup plus 1 tablespoon shortening
2 to 3 tablespoons cold water

One-Crust Pie; 10-inch

1⅓ cups all-purpose flour
½ teaspoon salt
¼ cup plus 3 tablespoons lard or ½ cup shortening
3 to 4 tablespoons cold water

Two-Crust Pie; 9-inch

2 cups all-purpose flour
1 teaspoon salt
⅔ cup lard or ⅔ cup plus 2 tablespoons shortening
4 to 5 tablespoons cold water

Two-Crust Pie; 10-inch

2⅔ cups all-purpose flour
1 teaspoon salt
¾ cup plus 2 tablespoons lard or 1 cup shortening
7 to 8 tablespoons cold water

Mix flour and salt. Cut in lard until particles are size of small peas. Sprinkle with water, 1 tablespoon at a time, tossing with fork until all flour is moistened and pastry almost cleans side of bowl (1 to 2 teaspoons water can be added if necessary).

Gather pastry into a ball; shape into flattened round on lightly floured cloth-covered surface. (For Two-Crust Pie, divide pastry in half and shape into 2 rounds.)

Roll pastry 2 inches larger than inverted pie plate with floured cloth-covered rolling pin. Fold pastry into fourths; unfold and ease into plate, pressing firmly against bottom and side.

For One-Crust Pie: Trim overhanging edge of pastry 1 inch from rim of plate. Fold and roll pastry under, even with plate. Flatten pastry evenly on rim of pie plate. Press firmly around edge with tines of fork, dipping fork into flour occasionally to prevent sticking. Or build up edge of pastry. Place index finger on inside of pastry edge and knuckles (or thumb and index finger) on outside. Pinch pastry into V shape; pinch again to sharpen. Fill and bake as directed in recipe.

For Baked Pie Shell: Heat oven to 475°. Prick bottom and side thoroughly with fork. Bake 8 to 10 minutes or until light brown; cool.

For Two-Crust Pie: Turn desired filling into pastry-lined pie plate. Trim overhanging edge of pastry ½ inch from rim of plate. Roll other round of pastry. Fold into fourths; cut slits so steam can escape.

Place over filling and unfold. Trim overhanging edge of pastry 1 inch from rim of plate. Fold and roll top edge under lower edge, pressing on rim to seal. Flatten pastry evenly on rim of pie plate. Press firmly around edge with tines of fork, dipping fork into flour occasionally to prevent sticking. Or build up edge of pastry. Place index finger on inside of pastry edge and knuckles (or thumb and index finger) on outside. Pinch pastry into V shape; pinch again to sharpen.

Apple-Praline Pie

Pastry for 10-inch Two-Crust Pie
   (page 42)
1 cup granulated sugar
2/3 cup chopped pecans
1/3 cup all-purpose flour
1 teaspoon ground cinnamon
1 teaspoon ground nutmeg
1/4 teaspoon salt
8 cups thinly sliced pared tart apples (about
   7 medium)
3 tablespoons butter or margarine
1/4 cup packed brown sugar
2 tablespoons half-and-half
Pecan halves

Heat oven to 425°. Prepare pastry. Mix granulated sugar, 2/3 cup pecans, the flour, cinnamon, nutmeg and salt in large bowl. Toss with apples. Turn into pastry-lined pie plate. Dot with butter. Cover with top crust; seal and flute. Cover edge with 2- to 3-inch strip of aluminum foil to prevent excessive browning; remove foil during last 15 minutes of baking.

Bake 50 to 60 minutes or until crust is brown and juice begins to bubble through slits in crust. Mix brown sugar and the half-and-half in 1-quart saucepan. Cook over low heat, stirring constantly, until sugar is melted. Spread over hot pie; sprinkle with pecan halves. **8 servings.**

Deep-dish Cherry-Berry Pie

Pastry for 9-inch One-Crust Pie (page 42)
3/4 cup sugar
1/2 cup all-purpose flour
2 1/3 cups fresh red tart cherries, pitted*
2 cups fresh strawberries, cut in half**
1 teaspoon grated orange peel
1 tablespoon orange juice
Red food color, if desired
1 tablespoon butter or margarine

Heat oven to 425°. Generously grease square pan, 9 × 9 × 2 inches, or deep-dish pie plate, 9 1/2 × 1 3/4 inches. Prepare pastry as directed—except roll into 10-inch square. Make cutouts near center so steam can escape. Mix sugar and flour in medium bowl; stir in cherries, strawberries, orange peel, orange juice and red food color. Turn into pan. Dot with butter. Fold pastry in half; place over fruit mixture. Fold edges of pastry just under inside edges of pan; press pastry to edges of pan. Bake about 55 minutes or until juice begins to bubble through cutouts in crust. Serve warm with whipping (heavy) cream if desired. **9 servings.**

*2 cans (about 16 ounces each) pitted red tart cherries, drained, can be substituted for the fresh cherries.

**2 cups frozen strawberries, thawed, drained and cut in half, can be substituted for the fresh strawberries.

Pear-Rhubarb Pie

*Pastry for 9-inch Two-Crust Pie
  (page 42)*
1 to 1¼ cups sugar
⅓ cup all-purpose flour
¼ teaspoon salt
*2½ cups pears, pared and diced
  (about 4)*
1½ cups 1-inch pieces rhubarb
2 tablespoons butter or margarine

Heat oven to 425°. Prepare pastry. Mix sugar, flour and salt in medium bowl. Toss with pears and rhubarb. Turn into pastry-lined pie plate. Dot with butter. Cover with top crust; seal and flute. Cover edge with 2- to 3-inch strip of aluminum foil to prevent excessive browning; remove foil during last 15 minutes of baking.

Bake 40 to 50 minutes or until crust is brown and juice begins to bubble through slits in crust. **8 servings.**

Upside-down Plum-Pecan Pie

¼ cup butter or margarine, softened
30 pecan halves (about ½ cup)
⅓ cup packed brown sugar
1 tablespoon corn syrup
*Pastry for 9-inch Two-Crust Pie
  (page 42)*
4 cups plum slices (about 1½ pounds)
½ cup granulated sugar
⅓ cup all-purpose flour
1 tablespoon lemon juice

Cut 15-inch circle from heavy-duty aluminum foil. Line pie plate, 9 × 1¼ inches, with foil circle, leaving 2 inches overhanging edge. Spread butter over foil lining. Place pecan halves, rounded sides down, on foil. Mix brown sugar and corn syrup. Drop by small spoonfuls evenly over pecans and buttered foil.

Heat oven to 450°. Prepare pastry. Roll one round pastry into 11-inch circle. Ease into pie plate over pecans and brown sugar mixture. Mix remaining ingredients; pour into pastry-lined plate. Roll other round of pastry into 12-inch circle. Fold into fourths; cut slits so steam can escape. Place over filling and unfold; seal and flute. Turn up overhanging foil to catch bubbling juices and to prevent crust from excessive browning. Bake 10 minutes.

Reduce oven temperature to 375°. Bake 35 to 40 minutes longer or until crust is brown and juice begins to bubble through slits in crust. Cool 5 minutes. Turn foil away from pastry. Invert pie onto heatproof serving plate; peel off foil. Serve warm. **8 servings.**

Upside-down Plum-Pecan Pie

Apricot-Mince Pie

Once actually made with minced beef, mincemeat now usually includes only fruits, nuts, spices, brandy or rum and sometimes beef suet. Mincemeat has been a favorite for centuries, especially at Thanksgiving and Christmas.

Pastry for 9-inch Two-Crust Pie (page 42)
1 cup dried apricots
1 tablespoon sugar
1 jar (27 ounces) mincemeat

Heat oven to 425°. Prepare pastry. Mix apricots and sugar in 1½-quart saucepan. Add just enough water to cover apricots. Heat to boiling over medium heat; reduce heat. Simmer uncovered about 20 minutes or until apricots are tender; drain.

Place apricots in pastry-lined pie plate. Spread with mincemeat. Cover with top crust; seal and flute. Cover edge with 2- to 3-inch strip of aluminum foil to prevent excessive browning; remove foil during last 15 minutes of baking. Bake 35 to 40 minutes or until crust is brown. **8 servings.**

Green Tomato Pie

New Englanders, from colonial days up to the present, have made this pie when an early frost forced them to pick green tomatoes. If you find yourself with a large green tomato harvest, comfort yourself with a slice of this traditional pie.

Pastry for 9-inch Two-Crust Pie (page 42)
1⅓ cups sugar
¼ cup plus 3 tablespoons all-purpose flour
1¼ teaspoons ground nutmeg or ground cinnamon
1 teaspoon salt
4 cups green tomato slices
1¼ teaspoons grated lemon peel
¼ cup lemon juice
1 tablespoon butter or margarine

Heat oven to 425°. Prepare pastry. Mix sugar, flour, nutmeg and salt. Toss with tomatoes, lemon peel and lemon juice. Turn into pastry-lined pie plate. Dot with butter. Cover with top crust; seal and flute. Cover edge with 2- to 3-inch strip of aluminum foil to prevent excessive browning; remove foil during last 15 minutes of baking.

Bake 35 to 40 minutes or until crust is brown and juice begins to bubble through slits in crust. Serve warm. **8 servings.**

Green Tomato Pie, Double-Crust Lemon Pie (page 48)

Double-Crust Lemon Pie

2 large lemons
2 teaspoons grated lemon peel
2 cups sugar
1 teaspoon salt
Pastry for 9-inch Two-Crust Pie
   (page 42)
4 eggs

Grate peel from lemons. Peel lemons, removing all white membrane. Cut lemons into very thin slices. Place lemon slices in medium bowl. Stir in lemon peel from lemons, 2 teaspoons lemon peel, sugar and salt; set aside.

Heat oven to 425°. Prepare pastry. Beat eggs thoroughly. Pour over lemon slices; mix well. Pour into pastry-lined pie plate. Cover with top crust; seal and flute. Cover edge with 2- to 3-inch strip of aluminum foil to prevent excessive browning; remove foil during last 15 minutes of baking.

Bake 45 to 50 minutes or until knife inserted 1 inch from edge comes out clean; cool. **8 servings.**

Coconut–Cottage Cheese Pie

Pastry for 9-inch One-Crust Pie (page 42)
3 eggs
¾ cup sugar
¾ cup milk
1 teaspoon grated lemon peel
1 container (12 ounces) small curd dry
   cottage cheese (1½ cups)
1¼ cups shredded coconut
½ teaspoon ground nutmeg

Heat oven to 425°. Prepare pastry. Beat eggs slightly in large bowl. Beat in sugar, milk, lemon peel and cottage cheese. Pour into pastry-lined pie plate. Sprinkle coconut and nutmeg over top. Cover edge with 2- to 3-inch strip of aluminum foil to prevent excessive browning; remove foil during last 15 minutes of baking.

Bake 25 to 30 minutes or until knife inserted 1 inch from edge comes out clean. Cool 15 minutes; refrigerate until chilled. Refrigerate any remaining pie. **8 servings.**

Sour Cream Pie

You may wonder why this Sour Cream Pie recipe doesn't call for any sour cream. As a matter of fact, it does—you make your own the old-fashioned way, by mixing lemon juice into half-and-half. It won't taste exactly like store-bought sour cream . . . but it will taste a bit like old-time America.

Pastry for 9-inch One-Crust Pie (page 42)
3 egg whites
2 tablespoons lemon juice
1¾ cups half-and-half
⅔ cup sugar
3 tablespoons all-purpose flour
¼ teaspoon salt
3 egg yolks, slightly beaten
2 teaspoons vanilla
Raspberry Sauce (right)

Move oven rack to lowest position. Heat oven to 425°. Prepare pastry. Beat egg whites in medium bowl until stiff. Mix lemon juice and half-and-half. Mix sugar, flour and salt in small bowl. Stir in half-and-half mixture, egg yolks and vanilla. Fold into egg whites. Pour into pastry-lined pie plate. Bake 10 minutes.

Reduce oven temperature to 325°. Bake about 30 minutes longer or until knife inserted 1 inch from edge comes out clean. Cool 15 minutes; refrigerate until chilled. Prepare Raspberry Sauce. Serve pie with warm Raspberry Sauce. Refrigerate any remaining pie. **8 servings.**

Raspberry Sauce

1 package (10 ounces) frozen raspberries in syrup, thawed, drained and syrup reserved
1 tablespoon cornstarch
½ cup grenadine syrup

Add enough water to reserved raspberry syrup to measure ⅔ cup. Stir cornstarch into syrup mixture in 1-quart saucepan. Heat to boiling, stirring constantly. Boil and stir 1 minute. Mix in raspberries and grenadine syrup.

Prune Custard Pie

Pastry for 9-inch One-Crust Pie (page 42)
3 eggs
¼ cup all-purpose flour
1 cup sugar
¼ teaspoon salt
⅛ teaspoon ground cinnamon
1½ cups chopped pitted prunes
1 cup milk
½ cup prune juice
1 teaspoon vanilla

Heat oven to 375°. Prepare pastry. Beat eggs slightly in medium bowl. Mix in flour, sugar, salt and cinnamon thoroughly. Stir in remaining ingredients. Pour into pastry-lined pie plate, distributing prunes evenly.

Bake 50 to 60 minutes or until knife inserted 1 inch from edge comes out clean. Cool 15 minutes; refrigerate until chilled. Serve with sweetened whipped cream if desired. Refrigerate any remaining pie. **8 servings.**

Pies weren't always just for dessert—they were eaten for breakfast and lunch, and they were even given to children in church to keep them quiet! Although we think of pie as the most American of foods, pies were, in fact, a European invention many centuries earlier. An English "pye" often had a meat filling covered by a pastry crust. These crusts (and the pans in which they were baked) were called "coffins," because they were deep and covered the sides of the pie. The pan shape we think of as standard today was developed by early American settlers; the shallow, sloped sides of the pan allowed the thrifty baker to stretch limited resources. When there was an abundance of fruit, however, deep-dish pies were baked to take advantage of the plenty. In later years, new types of pies came on the scene. Chiffon pies, cream pies, custard pies and angel pies have joined fruit pies among the ranks of the best-loved American desserts.

Pumpkin-Honey Pie

Pastry for 9-inch One-Crust Pie (page 42)
3 eggs
2 cups mashed cooked pumpkin*
¾ cup honey
½ cup milk
¼ cup whipping (heavy) cream
1½ teaspoons ground cinnamon
½ teaspoon salt
¼ teaspoon ground ginger
¼ teaspoon ground nutmeg

Heat oven to 400°. Prepare pastry. Beat eggs slightly in large bowl, using hand beater. Beat in remaining ingredients. Pour into pastry-lined pie plate. Cover edge with 2- to 3-inch strip of aluminum foil to prevent excessive browning; remove foil during last 15 minutes of baking.

Bake 50 to 55 minutes or until knife inserted 1 inch from edge comes out clean. Cool 15 minutes; refrigerate until chilled. Serve with sweetened whipped cream sprinkled with nutmeg if desired. Refrigerate any remaining pie. **8 servings.**

*1 can (16 ounces) pumpkin can be substituted for the mashed cooked pumpkin.

Pumpkin-Honey Pie, Sweet Potato–Pecan Pie (page 52)

Sweet Potato–Pecan Pie

Pecan Pastry (below)
3 eggs
1¾ cups mashed cooked sweet potatoes*
1 cup sugar
1 cup milk
2 tablespoons butter or margarine, melted
½ teaspoon salt
¼ teaspoon ground cinnamon
¼ teaspoon ground nutmeg
⅛ teaspoon ground cloves
½ cup chopped pecans

Heat oven to 425°. Prepare Pecan Pastry. Beat eggs slightly in large bowl, using hand beater. Beat in remaining ingredients except pecans. Pour into pastry-lined pie plate; sprinkle with pecans. Bake 15 minutes.

Reduce oven temperature to 350°. Bake about 45 minutes longer or until knife inserted in center comes out clean. Cool 15 minutes; refrigerate until chilled. Serve with sweetened whipped cream and additional pecans if desired. Refrigerate any remaining pie. **8 servings.**

*1¾ cups mashed canned sweet potatoes can be substituted for the mashed cooked sweet potatoes.

Pecan Pastry

1 cup all-purpose flour
½ teaspoon salt
⅓ cup lard or ⅓ cup plus 1 tablespoon
  shortening
2 tablespoons finely chopped pecans
2 to 3 tablespoons cold water

Mix flour and salt. Cut in lard until particles are size of small peas; stir in pecans. Sprinkle with water, 1 tablespoon at a time, tossing with fork until all flour is moistened and pastry almost cleans side of bowl (1 to 2 teaspoons water can be added if necessary).

Gather pastry into a ball; shape into flattened round on lightly floured cloth-covered surface. Roll pastry 2 inches larger than inverted pie plate with floured cloth-covered rolling pin.

Fold pastry into fourths; unfold and ease into plate, pressing firmly against bottom and side. Trim overhanging edge of pastry 1 inch from rim of plate. Fold and roll pastry under, even with plate; build up a high edge and flute.

Storage of produce presented a problem in the age before iceboxes and commercially frozen or canned fruits. "Putting up" fruits and vegetables was a summer and autumn tradition. Early settlers also found that root vegetables could be successfully stored over the winter in cool, dark root cellars. Pumpkins, widely grown in the Northeast, were used in many recipes, including what may be our most traditional Thanksgiving pie. Down South, abundant sweet potatoes gained significantly in popularity during the Civil War. With food shortages, the plentiful and easily stored root vegetables were used in everything from main dishes to desserts. While using such practical pie fillings as sweet potato and pumpkin may have been a virtue born of necessity, these pies have become perennial favorites.

Shaker Sugar Pie

Although this particular recipe has the Shaker touch (notice the traditional Shaker use of rose flower water), variations on the sugar pie theme were also enjoyed by pie lovers from Indiana to New England to the South.

Pastry for 9-inch One-Crust Pie (page 42)
1 cup packed brown sugar
½ cup butter or margarine, softened
2 tablespoons all-purpose flour
1½ cups whipping (heavy) cream
1 teaspoon rose flower water or vanilla
1 egg
Ground nutmeg

Heat oven to 450°. Prepare pastry. Mix brown sugar, butter and flour until well blended; spread in pastry shell. Beat whipping cream, rose flower water and egg with hand beater until well blended. Pour over brown sugar mixture. Sprinkle with nutmeg. Bake 10 minutes.

Reduce oven temperature to 350°. Bake 25 to 30 minutes longer or until knife inserted in center comes out clean. Cool 15 minutes; refrigerate until chilled. Refrigerate any remaining pie. **12 servings.**

Marlborough Pie

This creamy pie is in season all year-'round. It uses applesauce rather than fresh apples. Marlborough Pie is sometimes made with grated or chopped apples, and this together with the addition of whipping cream are what make it distinctively "Marlborough."

Pastry for 9-inch One-Crust Pie (page 42)
4 eggs
¾ cup sugar
¾ cup whipping (heavy) cream
⅔ cup chunky applesauce
2 tablespoons lemon juice
2 tablespoons butter or margarine, melted
½ teaspoon salt
½ teaspoon ground nutmeg

Heat oven to 450°. Prepare pastry. Beat eggs slightly in medium bowl. Mix in remaining ingredients. Pour into pastry-lined pie plate. Cover edge with 2- to 3-inch strip of aluminum foil to prevent excess browning; remove foil during last 15 minutes of baking. Bake 15 minutes.

Reduce oven temperature to 325°. Bake 20 to 25 minutes longer or until knife inserted 1 inch from edge comes out clean. Cool 15 minutes; refrigerate at least 1 hour. Refrigerate any remaining pie. **8 servings.**

Fried Jam Pies

These delicious, hand-held pastries were a popular way to keep children quiet during long church services.

Pastry for 9-inch Two-Crust Pie (page 42)
About ¾ cup jam, jelly or preserves
¾ cup shortening
Powdered sugar

Prepare pastry. Divide evenly into 12 pieces. Roll each piece into ball; flatten slightly (do not overwork pastry). Roll each ball into 4½-inch circle on lightly floured cloth-covered surface with floured cloth-covered rolling pin. Place 1 tablespoon jam on half of each circle. Moisten edge of pastry; fold pastry over jam and seal edges with fork.

Heat the shortening in 10-inch skillet over medium heat until melted. Fry pies about 2 minutes on each side or until golden brown. Drain on paper towels; cool slightly. Sprinkle with powdered sugar. **12 pies.**

Chocolate Angel Pie

Meringue makes a light, crisp and slightly chewy shell for angel pies.

4 egg whites
¼ teaspoon cream of tartar
⅛ teaspoon salt
¾ cup sugar
1 teaspoon vanilla
½ cup chopped pecans
1 package (6 ounces) semisweet chocolate chips
¼ cup whipping (heavy) cream
1½ teaspoons vanilla
1½ cups whipping (heavy) cream

Heat oven to 275°. Generously grease pie plate, 9 × 1¼ inches; grease top edge of pie plate. Beat egg whites, cream of tartar and salt in small bowl until foamy. Beat in sugar, 1 tablespoon at a time; continue beating until stiff and glossy. Do not underbeat. Beat in vanilla; fold in pecans. Spread on bottom and up side of pie plate, using back of spoon and building up 1-inch edge to form shell. Bake 1½ hours. Turn oven off. Leave shell in oven with door closed 1 hour. Remove from oven and cool completely.

Heat chocolate chips and ¼ cup whipping cream in saucepan over low heat, stirring frequently, until chocolate is melted. Cool 30 minutes.

Stir in vanilla. Beat 1½ cups whipping cream in chilled medium bowl until stiff. Fold chocolate mixture into whipped cream. Spoon into meringue shell. Cover and refrigerate at least 12 hours but no longer than 24 hours. Garnish with whipped cream, chopped nuts or grated chocolate if desired. Refrigerate any remaining pie. **12 servings.**

Fried Jam Pies, Deep-dish Cherry-Berry Pie (page 43)

Mock Apple Pie

You won't find a single apple in this pie. Instead, crackers magically turn into apples! Actually, the crackers stay crackers, but the result just about duplicates the flavor and texture of fresh apple pie. This recipe, also known as Crazy Apple Pie, was popularized on the back of cracker boxes.

2½ cups water
1¾ cups sugar
2½ teaspoons cream of tartar
30 round buttery crackers
Pastry for 9-inch Two-Crust Pie (page 42)
1 teaspoon grated lemon peel
1 tablespoon plus 1 teaspoon lemon juice
½ teaspoon ground cinnamon
Butter or margarine

Mix water, sugar and cream of tartar in 3-quart saucepan. Heat to boiling, stirring occasionally. Boil 2 minutes. Add crackers; cool.

Heat oven to 425°. Prepare pastry. Carefully pour cracker mixture into pastry-lined pie plate. Sprinkle with lemon peel, lemon juice and cinnamon; dot with butter. Cover with top crust, seal and flute. Bake 30 to 35 minutes or until crust is deep golden brown. **8 servings.**

Streusel Peach Tarts

Pastry for 9-inch Two-Crust Pie (page 42)
½ teaspoon ground nutmeg
½ cup sugar
2 tablespoons all-purpose flour
2 tablespoons butter or margarine
¼ teaspoon ground cinnamon
⅛ teaspoon ground nutmeg
*4 fresh peaches, peeled, pitted and halved**

Heat oven to 350°. Prepare pastry as directed—except stir in ½ teaspoon nutmeg with the flour. Roll pastry into 15-inch circle. Cut into eight 4½-inch circles. Fit circles into individual tart pans or 6-ounce custard cups, making pleats so pastry will fit closely; do not prick.

Mix sugar, flour, butter, cinnamon and ⅛ teaspoon nutmeg until crumbly. Sprinkle half of the crumbly mixture in tart shells. Place 1 peach half, rounded side up, in each tart shell. Sprinkle remaining crumbly mixture over peaches. Bake 25 to 30 minutes or until light brown. Serve warm with whipping (heavy) cream if desired. **8 tarts.**

**8 canned peach halves, drained, can be substituted for the fresh peach halves.*

Banana Cream Tart

If you are going to garnish with extra banana slices, dip them in lemon juice and put them on the tart just before serving to keep them fresh-looking.

½ cup granulated sugar
3 tablespoons cornstarch
¼ teaspoon salt
2¼ cups milk
3 egg yolks
1 tablespoon butter or margarine, softened
1 teaspoon vanilla
Pastry for 9-inch One-Crust Pie (page 42)
2 bananas
½ cup whipping (heavy) cream
1 tablespoon powdered sugar

Mix granulated sugar, cornstarch and salt in 1½-quart saucepan. Gradually stir in milk. Cook over medium heat, stirring constantly, until mixture thickens and boils. Boil and stir 1 minute. Beat egg yolks until well blended. Stir at least half of the hot mixture gradually into egg yolks. Stir into hot mixture in saucepan. Boil and stir 1 minute; remove from heat. Stir in butter and vanilla. Press plastic wrap onto filling in saucepan. Refrigerate 1 hour.

Heat oven to 475°. Prepare pastry as directed—except roll into 11-inch circle. Fold pastry into fourths; unfold and ease into tart pan, 9 × 1 inch, pressing firmly against bottom and side. Trim any excess pastry by pressing against edge of pan. Prick bottom and side thoroughly with fork. Bake 10 to 12 minutes or until light brown; cool.

Spread ½ cup of the filling in tart shell. Slice bananas over filling. Spread remaining filling over bananas. Beat whipping cream and powdered sugar in chilled small bowl until stiff; spread over filling. Refrigerate at least 2 hours but no longer than 48 hours. Garnish with additional banana slices if desired. Refrigerate any remaining tart. **8 servings.**

Red Currant–glazed Grape Tart

1½ cups all-purpose flour
⅔ cup butter or margarine, softened
⅓ cup sugar
3 cups seedless red grape halves
1 envelope unflavored gelatin
¼ cup orange juice
1 jar (10 ounces) red currant jelly

Heat oven to 400°. Mix flour, butter and sugar until crumbly. Press firmly and evenly in bottom of 12-inch pizza pan. Bake 10 to 15 minutes or until light brown; cool.

Place grapes evenly over crust. Sprinkle gelatin on orange juice in 1-quart saucepan to soften. Stir in jelly. Heat over medium heat, stirring constantly, until gelatin is dissolved and jelly is melted. Spoon over grapes. Refrigerate about 1½ hours or until set. Serve with sweetened whipped cream if desired. **10 to 12 servings.**

Fresh Blueberry Tart

Vinegar may seem like an unusual ingredient, but it actually contributes to the wonderfully flaky texture of this tart crust.

1 cup all-purpose flour
2 tablespoons granulated sugar
⅛ teaspoon salt
½ cup butter or margarine
1 tablespoon white vinegar
1 cup granulated sugar
2 tablespoons all-purpose flour
¼ teaspoon ground cinnamon
3 cups blueberries
2 tablespoons powdered sugar

Mix 1 cup flour, 2 tablespoons granulated sugar and the salt. Cut in butter. Stir in vinegar until dough forms. Press dough evenly on bottom and 1 inch up side of ungreased springform pan, 9 × 3 inches, or square pan, 8 × 8 × 2 inches. (Be sure there are no thin areas at bottom seam of springform pan.) Refrigerate at least 15 minutes.

Heat oven to 400°. Mix 1 cup granulated sugar, 2 tablespoons flour and the cinnamon. Reserve 1 cup of the largest blueberries. Gently stir remaining blueberries into sugar mixture. Spread evenly in tart shell. Bake 50 to 60 minutes or until crust is golden brown. Sprinkle with reserved berries and powdered sugar; cool. Loosen tart from side of pan; remove side of pan. **8 servings.**

Burnt Sugar— Almond Tarts

1 cup sugar
½ cup boiling water
3 tablespoons butter or margarine
⅔ cup whipping (heavy) cream
Pastry for 9-inch One-Crust Pie (page 42)
⅔ cup slivered almonds, toasted (see Note, page 26)
½ cup sugar
½ teaspoon vanilla
2 eggs

Heat 1 cup sugar in 10-inch heavy skillet over medium-low heat until sugar begins to melt. Continue cooking, stirring occasionally, until completely melted and medium brown; remove from heat. Slowly stir in boiling water, mixing thoroughly. (If any lumps remain, return to heat until melted.) Cool 5 minutes; stir in butter. Stir in whipping cream until well blended; cool.

Move oven rack to lowest position. Heat oven to 350°. Prepare pastry as directed—except roll into 15-inch circle. Cut into eight 4½-inch circles. Reroll pastry scraps; cut into 4½-inch circle. Fit circles into individual tart pans or 6-ounce custard cups, making pleats so pastry will fit closely; do not prick. Sprinkle almonds in tart shells.

Beat ½ cup sugar, the vanilla, eggs and whipping cream mixture. Pour about ¼ cup mixture into each tart shell. Bake 28 to 33 minutes or until set. Cool 15 minutes; remove from pans. Serve warm or chilled. **9 tarts.**

Chess Tart

Chess tarts owe their name to the fact that at one time the filling included cheese. The name chess (derived from "cheese") endures, although the cheese has been replaced by a lemon-flavored mixture.

Pastry for 9-inch One-Crust Pie (page 42)
4 eggs
1½ cups sugar
½ cup butter or margarine, softened
2 tablespoons yellow cornmeal
2 tablespoons half-and-half
2 tablespoons lemon juice
2 teaspoons vanilla
Dash of salt

Heat oven to 325°. Prepare pastry. Beat eggs, sugar and butter 3 minutes in medium bowl on high speed. Beat in remaining ingredients (mixture will look curdled). Pour into pastry-lined pie plate. Bake about 1 hour or until set. Cool 15 minutes; refrigerate until chilled. Refrigerate any remaining tart. **8 servings.**

Lemon Curd Tart

Pastry for 9-inch One-Crust Pie (page 42)
3 eggs
1 cup sugar
¾ cup butter or margarine, softened
½ cup lemon juice
1 tablespoon grated lemon peel

Heat oven to 475°. Prepare pastry as directed—except roll into 11-inch circle. Fold pastry into fourths; unfold and ease into tart pan, 9 × 1 inch, pressing firmly against bottom and side. Trim any excess pastry by pressing against edge of pan. Prick bottom and side thoroughly with fork. Bake 8 to 10 minutes or until light brown; cool.

Beat eggs in 1½-quart saucepan until fluffy. Mix in remaining ingredients. Cook over medium-low heat 8 to 10 minutes, stirring constantly, until mixture is thick enough to coat a metal spoon; cool slightly. Pour into tart shell. Cover and refrigerate at least 2 hours but no longer than 48 hours. Serve with sweetened whipped cream and fresh fruit if desired. Refrigerate any remaining tart. **12 servings.**

Chocolate-Hazelnut Tart

The abundance of hazelnuts, or "filberts," as they are also called, led to their frequent use in old-time recipes. They are still quite popular; if you can't find them in your usual grocery store, try a gourmet shop.

Pastry for 9-inch One-Crust Pie (page 42)
⅓ cup butter or margarine
2 ounces unsweetened chocolate
3 eggs
⅔ cup sugar
½ teaspoon salt
1 cup corn syrup
1 cup hazelnuts, skinned and coarsely chopped

Move oven rack to lowest position. Heat oven to 475°. Prepare pastry as directed—except roll into 12-inch circle. Fold pastry into fourths; unfold and ease into springform pan, 9 × 3 inches, pressing firmly against bottom and side. Prick bottom and side thoroughly with fork. Bake 5 minutes; cool.

Reduce oven temperature to 350°. Heat butter and chocolate over low heat, stirring constantly, until chocolate is melted; cool slightly. Beat eggs, sugar, salt, chocolate mixture and corn syrup in medium bowl using hand beater. Stir in hazelnuts. Pour into pastry-lined pan.

Bake 65 to 70 minutes or until set; cool 10 minutes. Loosen tart from side of pan; remove side of pan. Serve with sweetened whipped cream if desired. Refrigerate any remaining tart. **12 servings.**

Note: To skin hazelnuts, heat oven to 275°. Spread hazelnuts in single layer in ungreased shallow pan. Bake 20 to 25 minutes, shaking pan occasionally, until skins crack. Immediately wrap nuts in towel; let steam about 10 minutes. Rub nuts in towel until skins flake off.

CHAPTER FOUR
Nostalgic Custards and Puddings

Custards and puddings are classic "comfort foods." Simple and hearty, they hearken back to early colonial days when puddings were considered heavier additions to the meal instead of just dessert. They also remind us of favorite childhood lunches. Remember delicious Bread-and-Butter Pudding (page 69), smooth custard or Chocolate Pudding (page 65) with a dollop of whipped cream? These can be more than memories, and you will find that making your own pudding is easier than you might think.

Puddings and custards are extraordinarily versatile; they are wonderful plain, but you can dress them up quickly with fruit, whipped cream or toasted nuts. Serve them with delicate ladyfingers for a sophisticated treat. Custard is also the base for other recipes such as Layered Fruit Dessert (page 87). You can be creative and use a homemade custard to fill Cream Puffs (page 96) or Eclairs (page 97).

Since colonial days, New Englanders have favored such hearty desserts as Hasty Pudding (page 65). This is traditional American cooking at its most basic, combining quick preparation with plain ingredients—the primary ingredient is native corn. But we also adore such elegant desserts as the light and airy Apricot Mousse (page 74), and the coffee shop and diner favorites such as Tapioca Pudding (page 70) and Brown Rice Pudding (page 70). These desserts are well loved anytime, from the most casual Saturday lunch to a formal dinner party.

Bread-and-Butter Pudding (page 69),
Baked Honey Custard (page 65)

Creamy Stirred Custard

This classic custard will stir up delicious memories of days gone by. It is a wonderfully simple treat served as is, but it's versatile and lends itself to use in many other desserts, among them parfaits, icebox desserts and as dessert sauces. It is used in Layered Fruit Dessert (page 87).

3 eggs
⅓ cup sugar
Dash of salt
2½ cups milk
1 teaspoon vanilla

Beat eggs slightly in 2-quart heavy saucepan. Stir in sugar and salt. Gradually stir in milk. Cook over medium heat 15 to 20 minutes, stirring constantly, until mixture just coats a metal spoon; remove from heat. Stir in vanilla. Place saucepan in cold water until custard is cool. (If custard curdles, beat vigorously with hand beater until smooth.) Cover and refrigerate at least 2 hours. Refrigerate any remaining custard. **5 servings.**

Brandy Flans

¾ cup sugar
2 tablespoons water
½ cup sugar
2 eggs, slightly beaten
2 tablespoons brandy or 2 teaspoons brandy flavoring
½ teaspoon vanilla
¼ teaspoon ground nutmeg
¼ teaspoon ground cinnamon
¼ teaspoon ground allspice
Dash of salt
2 cups milk, scalded and cooled

Heat ¾ cup sugar in heavy 1-quart saucepan over low heat, stirring constantly, until sugar is melted and golden brown. Gradually stir in water. Divide syrup evenly among six 6-ounce custard cups. Allow syrup to harden in cups about 10 minutes.

Heat oven to 350°. Mix ½ cup sugar, the eggs, brandy, vanilla, nutmeg, cinnamon, allspice and salt. Gradually stir in milk. Pour custard mixture over syrup. Place cups in rectangular pan, 13 × 9 × 2 inches, on oven rack. Pour very hot water into pan to within ½ inch of tops of cups.

Baked about 45 minutes or until knife inserted halfway between center and edge comes out clean. Remove cups from water. Refrigerate until chilled; unmold at serving time. **6 servings.**

Baked Honey Custard

2 eggs
⅓ cup honey
¼ teaspoon salt
½ teaspoon vanilla
1¾ cups milk, scalded
Ground nutmeg

Heat oven to 350°. Beat eggs slightly in medium bowl. Mix in honey, salt and vanilla. Gradually stir in milk. Pour into five 6-ounce custard cups. Sprinkle with nutmeg. Place cups in baking pan on oven rack; pour very hot water into pan to within ½ inch of tops of cups.

Bake 40 to 50 minutes or until knife inserted halfway between center and edge comes out clean. Remove cups from water. Serve warm or cover and refrigerate about 3 hours or until chilled. Refrigerate any remaining custard. **5 servings.**

Chocolate Pudding

½ cup sugar
⅓ cup cocoa
2 tablespoons cornstarch
⅛ teaspoon salt
2 cups milk
2 egg yolks, slightly beaten
2 tablespoons butter or margarine
2 teaspoons vanilla

Mix sugar, cocoa, cornstarch and salt in 2-quart saucepan. Gradually stir in milk. Cook over medium heat, stirring constantly, until mixture thickens and boils. Boil and stir 1 minute.

Gradually stir at least half of the hot mixture into egg yolks; stir into hot mixture in saucepan.

Heat to boiling, stirring constantly. Boil and stir 1 minute; remove from heat. Stir in butter and vanilla. Pour into dessert dishes. Serve warm, or cover and refrigerate about 2 hours or until chilled. Refrigerate any remaining pudding. **4 servings.**

Hasty Pudding

Hasty Pudding has been a favorite dessert in New England since the very earliest colonial days. It's a quick, simple pudding, the perfect "comfort food" for those cold winter days when all you want to do is curl up with a cup of tea, a book and something sweet to eat. Hasty Pudding was traditionally served with molasses before we had the luxury of granulated cane or beet sugar

¾ cup yellow cornmeal
¾ teaspoon salt
¾ cup cold water
2½ cups boiling water
Butter, margarine or half-and-half
Molasses or sugar

Mix cornmeal, salt and cold water in 2-quart saucepan. Gradually stir in boiling water. Cook over medium heat, stirring constantly, until mixture thickens and boils; reduce heat to low. Cover and cook 10 minutes. Serve warm with butter and molasses. **4 servings.**

Snow Mound Pudding with Lemon Sauce

4 egg whites
3/4 cup sugar
1/2 cup shortening
1 cup all-purpose flour
2 teaspoons baking powder
1/8 teaspoon salt
2/3 cup milk
2 tablespoons lemon juice
1 cup soft white bread crumbs
Lemon Sauce (right)

Generously butter 9-cup mold. Beat egg whites until stiff. Beat sugar and shortening in large bowl until light and fluffy. Stir in flour, baking powder and salt alternately with milk and lemon juice. Stir in bread crumbs. Fold in egg whites. Pour into mold. Cover tightly with aluminum foil.

Place mold on rack in Dutch oven or steamer; pour boiling water into Dutch oven halfway up mold. Cover Dutch oven. Keep water boiling over low heat about 1 hour or until toothpick inserted in center of pudding comes out clean. Serve hot with Lemon Sauce. **6 to 8 servings.**

Lemon Sauce

1/2 cup sugar
1 tablespoon cornstarch
Dash of salt
1 cup water
1 tablespoon butter or margarine
1 teaspoon grated lemon peel
1 1/2 tablespoons lemon juice

Mix sugar, cornstarch and salt in saucepan. Gradually stir in water. Cook over medium heat, stirring constantly, until mixture thickens and boils. Boil and stir 1 minute; remove from heat. Stir in remaining ingredients.

Tart Lemon Pudding

2 cups sugar
1/2 cup cornstarch
2 cups water
4 egg yolks, slightly beaten
1/4 cup butter or margarine
2 teaspoons grated lemon peel
2/3 cup lemon juice

Mix sugar and cornstarch in 2-quart saucepan. Gradually stir in water. Cook over medium heat, stirring constantly, until mixture thickens and boils. Boil and stir 1 minute.

Gradually stir at least half the hot mixture into egg yolks; stir into hot mixture in saucepan. Heat to boiling, stirring constantly. Boil and stir 2 minutes; remove from heat. Stir in butter, lemon peel and lemon juice. Pour into dessert dishes; refrigerate about 2 hours or until chilled. Refrigerate any remaining pudding. **4 servings.**

Tart Lemon Pudding

Steamed Fig Pudding

1 cup boiling water
1 cup finely chopped dried figs
2 tablespoons butter or margarine
1½ cups all-purpose flour
1 cup sugar
1 teaspoon baking soda
1 teaspoon salt
1 cup chopped nuts
1 egg
Creamy Sauce (below)

Generously grease 6-cup ovenproof mold. Pour boiling water over figs in small bowl; stir in butter. Mix flour, sugar, baking soda, salt and nuts in medium bowl. Stir in fig mixture and egg. Pour into mold. Cover with aluminum foil.

Place mold on rack in Dutch oven or steamer. Pour boiling water into Dutch oven halfway up mold. Cover Dutch oven and keep water boiling over low heat 2 hours or until toothpick inserted in center of pudding comes out clean. Remove mold from Dutch oven. Let stand 5 minutes; unmold. Prepare Creamy Sauce. Serve warm pudding with Creamy Sauce. **8 servings.**

Creamy Sauce

¾ cup powdered sugar
¾ cup butter or margarine, softened
¾ cup whipping (heavy) cream

Beat powdered sugar and butter in 1-quart saucepan until smooth and creamy. Stir in whipping cream. Heat to boiling, stirring occasionally. Serve immediately.

Bread-and-Butter Pudding

8 slices French bread, each ½ inch thick
2 tablespoons butter or margarine, softened
½ teaspoon ground cinnamon
3 eggs
⅔ cup sugar
1 teaspoon vanilla
Dash of salt
2½ cups milk, scalded and cooled

Heat oven to 350°. Butter 1½-quart casserole. Spread one side of each slice bread with butter. Layer bread slices, buttered sides up, in casserole; sprinkle with cinnamon. Beat eggs slightly in medium bowl; mix in sugar, vanilla and salt. Stir in milk; pour over bread.

Place casserole in pan of very hot water (1 inch deep). Cover casserole loosely with aluminum foil. Bake 20 minutes; remove foil. Continue baking 35 to 40 minutes longer or until knife inserted 1 inch from edge of casserole comes out clean. (Cover with foil if top gets too brown.)

Remove casserole from hot water. Sprinkle with powdered sugar if desired. Serve warm. Refrigerate any remaining pudding. **8 servings.**

Brown Rice Pudding

¼ cup uncooked brown rice
⅔ cup water
2 eggs or 4 egg yolks
½ cup sugar
¼ teaspoon salt
1 teaspoon vanilla
2 cups milk
½ cup raisins
Ground nutmeg

Stir together brown rice and water in 2-quart saucepan. Heat to boiling, stirring once or twice; reduce heat. Cover and simmer 45 to 50 minutes or until tender. (Do not lift cover or stir.)

Heat oven to 325°. Beat eggs in ungreased 1½-quart casserole. Stir in sugar, salt, vanilla, milk, hot rice and raisins. Sprinkle with nutmeg. Bake 50 to 60 minutes, stirring occasionally, until knife inserted halfway between center and edge comes out clean. Serve warm or cover and refrigerate about 3 hours or until chilled.

Serve with whipping (heavy) cream if desired. Refrigerate any remaining pudding. **6 to 8 servings.**

Tapioca Pudding

If pearl tapioca is not to be found at your grocery store, try a health-food store or gourmet shop. Like regular tapioca, it is a starch made from the root of the manioc plant. It has the texture and appearance of small, translucent pearls.

½ cup water
¼ cup uncooked pearl tapioca
2 cups milk
2 eggs
¼ cup sugar
⅛ teaspoon salt
1 teaspoon vanilla
1½ teaspoons butter or margarine

Pour water over tapioca; let stand 1 hour. Drain tapioca. Mix tapioca and milk in top of double boiler. Cover and cook over gently boiling water about 1 hour, stirring occasionally, until tapioca is transparent.

Heat oven to 325° Beat eggs, sugar, salt and vanilla. Gradually stir at least half of the hot tapioca mixture into egg mixture; stir into hot tapioca mixture in double boiler. Stir in butter. Pour into ungreased 1-quart casserole. Bake uncovered about 35 minutes or until knife inserted in center comes out clean. Serve warm, or cover and refrigerate about 3 hours or until chilled. Refrigerate any remaining pudding. **6 servings.**

Hot Fudge Sundae Cake

1 cup all-purpose flour
¾ cup granulated sugar
2 tablespoons cocoa
2 teaspoons baking powder
¼ teaspoon salt
½ cup milk
2 tablespoons vegetable oil
1 teaspoon vanilla
1 cup chopped nuts
1 cup packed brown sugar
¼ cup cocoa
1¾ cups very hot water
Ice cream

Heat oven to 350°. Mix flour, granulated sugar, 2 tablespoons cocoa, the baking powder and salt in ungreased square pan, 9 × 9 × 2 inches. Mix in milk, oil and vanilla with fork until smooth. Stir in nuts. Spread evenly. Sprinkle with brown sugar and ¼ cup cocoa. Pour hot water over batter.

Bake 40 minutes. While warm, spoon into dessert dishes and top with ice cream. Spoon sauce from pan over each serving. **9 servings.**

Maple Sugar Custard Soufflé

3 tablespoons butter or margarine
¼ cup all-purpose flour
¼ teaspoon ground nutmeg
1 cup milk
4 eggs, separated
¼ cup maple sugar or packed brown sugar

Heat butter in 2-quart saucepan over medium heat until melted. Stir in flour and nutmeg; remove from heat. Stir in milk. Heat to boiling, stirring constantly. Boil and stir about 1 minute or until thickened and smooth.

Beat egg yolks and maple sugar slightly in small bowl. Beat in about one-third of the milk mixture; stir into milk mixture in saucepan. Cool slightly.

Heat oven to 350°. Butter 6-cup soufflé dish. Beat egg whites in medium bowl until stiff. Do not underbeat. Stir about one-fourth of the egg whites into milk mixture; fold in remaining egg whites. Carefully pour into soufflé dish. Bake about 45 minutes or until set. Serve immediately and, if desired, with maple sugar. **6 servings.**

DESSERTS THEN

Maple syrup and maple sugar were the sole sweeteners used by Native Americans of the Northeast. Maple syrup can only be produced in the northern United States and nearby areas of Canada, due to temperature requirements. Settlers in the Northeast also used maple syrup extensively, but they began to use other sweeteners during the seventeenth century, as they became available. Even with the importation of molasses and cane sugar, however, maple syrup remained the most widely used sweetener right through the nineteenth century. It was the least expensive sweetener and many northerners felt that it was wrong to use molasses and cane sugar which were produced by slaves.

Golden Cottage Pudding

1½ cups cake flour or 1¼ cups all-purpose flour
1½ cups finely shredded carrots
1 cup sugar
⅓ cup shortening
¾ cup milk
1½ teaspoons baking powder
1 teaspoon lemon extract
½ teaspoon salt
1 egg
Golden Sauce (below)

Heat oven to 350°. Grease and flour square pan, 8 × 8 × 2 or 9 × 9 × 2 inches. Mix all ingredients except Golden Sauce on low speed 30 seconds, scraping bowl constantly. Beat on medium speed 3 minutes, scraping bowl occasionally. Pour into pan.

Bake 35 minutes or until toothpick inserted in center comes out clean. Prepare Golden Sauce. Serve warm pudding cake with Golden Sauce. **9 servings.**

Golden Sauce

1 cup sugar
¼ cup all-purpose flour
1½ cups boiling water
¼ cup butter or margarine
3 tablespoons finely shredded carrot
2 tablespoons lemon juice
2 tablespoons orange juice

Mix sugar and flour in 2-quart saucepan. Gradually stir in boiling water. Cook over medium heat, stirring constantly, until mixture thickens and boils. Boil and stir 1 minute; remove from heat. Stir in remaining ingredients. Serve immediately.

Strawberry-Rhubarb Flummery

Flummeries were originally thickened with oatmeal, although we now use cornstarch or flour. They were particularly popular among Shakers.

3 cups ½-inch pieces fresh rhubarb*
1 cup sugar
¼ cup cold water
3 tablespoons cornstarch
1 cup sliced fresh strawberries**
Few drops red food color
Whipping (heavy) cream

Heat rhubarb, sugar and 1 tablespoon of the water to boiling in 2-quart saucepan; reduce heat. Simmer uncovered about 5 minutes, stirring occasionally, until rhubarb is tender. Mix cornstarch and remaining water; stir into rhubarb mixture. Heat to boiling, stirring constantly. Boil and stir 1 minute. Stir in strawberries and food color. Spoon into dessert dishes. Cover and refrigerate about 2 hours or until chilled. Serve with whipping cream. **4 servings.**

*1 package (16 ounces) frozen unsweetened rhubarb, thawed and drained, can be substituted for the fresh rhubarb.

**1 package (10 ounces) frozen strawberries, thawed and drained, can be substituted for the fresh strawberries.

Golden Cottage Pudding

Apricot Mousse

2 cups peeled, sliced fresh apricots (about
    6 medium)*
1/4 cup sugar
2 envelopes unflavored gelatin
4 eggs
3 egg yolks
1/4 cup brandy or 2 teaspoons brandy
    flavoring
1/4 teaspoon almond extract
2 cups whipping (heavy) cream
Sweetened whipped cream

Place apricots in blender. Cover and blend on high speed about 1 minute or until smooth. Mix sugar and gelatin in 2-quart saucepan.

Beat eggs and egg yolks on high speed about 5 minutes or until thick and lemon colored. Stir eggs into gelatin mixture. Heat to boiling over medium heat, stirring constantly; remove from heat. Stir in apricot puree, brandy and almond extract. Refrigerate just until mixture mounds slightly when dropped from a spoon.

Beat whipping cream in chilled large bowl until stiff. Fold apricot mixture into whipped cream. Pour into 8-cup mold. Refrigerate until firm, at least 4 hours; unmold. Serve with sweetened whipped cream. Refrigerate any remaining mousse. **12 servings.**

1 can (30 ounces) apricot halves, drained, can be substituted for the 2 cups fresh apricot slices.

Rice Custard Cream with Strawberries

3 cups boiling water
1/2 cup uncooked medium grain rice
1 3/4 cups milk
1 envelope unflavored gelatin
2 tablespoons cold water
1/4 cup sugar
1 teaspoon vanilla
1 cup whipping (heavy) cream
2 cups sliced strawberries

Pour boiling water over rice in 2-quart saucepan. Let stand uncovered 10 minutes; drain. Heat rice and milk to boiling over medium heat, stirring occasionally; reduce heat. Simmer uncovered 20 minutes, stirring occasionally.

Sprinkle gelatin on cold water to soften; stir into rice mixture. Stir in sugar and vanilla. Refrigerate about 40 minutes or until chilled.

Beat whipping cream in chilled medium bowl until stiff; fold in rice mixture. Fold in strawberries. Spoon into dessert dishes. Refrigerate any remaining dessert. **8 servings.**

Rice Custard Cream with Strawberries

CHAPTER FIVE
Icebox Desserts

Even though we use refrigerators now, our grandparents remember the days when foods were kept cold in the icebox. The iceman would deliver large blocks of ice that slowly melted into the drip pan, cooling the air in the icebox. The drip pan had to be emptied occasionally so it wouldn't spill over. There's something thrilling about a cold dessert, whether it's a gorgeous molded dessert, a wonderfully easy trifle or a rich, creamy ice cream. Perhaps our excitement stems from the anticipation—waiting for those fabulous desserts to come out of the icebox.

One of our favorite icebox desserts, the charlotte russe, has set a standard for elegance since it was created in the nineteenth century. The combination of textures, smooth cream with delicate cake, and its beautiful molded appearance will crumble even the most steadfast dieter's resolve. That all-American favorite, ice cream, has been a national passion since it was popularized by Dolley Madison in the early 1800s. Store-bought ice cream is delicious, of course, but making your own ice cream presents so many opportunities to experiment with additions such as fruits, nuts and flavored extracts. The fresh, natural ingredients of homemade ice cream make a world of difference. Just think—Philadelphia Ice Cream (page 93) is made today almost exactly as it was in Dolley Madison's day; why fiddle with perfection?

Many of these recipes are perfect for entertaining because they're elegant and conveniently made ahead of serving. You'll find that they are great for more casual meals, too. You can even involve children in preparing such favorites as ice cream. Cranking an ice cream freezer is great fun, and it has such sweet rewards.

Chocolate-Apricot Charlotte Russe (page 80),
Ginger-Cream Parfaits (page 85)

Chocolate-Apricot Charlotte Russe

Elegant and sinfully delicious, the charlotte russe is a timeless classic. It was invented by Antonin Carême, one of the grand French chefs of the nineteenth century.

About ¼ Chocolate Angel Food Cake
(page 38)
½ cup sugar
¼ teaspoon salt
4 egg yolks, slightly beaten
1 envelope unflavored gelatin
2 cups milk
1 cup whipping (heavy) cream
1 teaspoon vanilla
Apricot Sauce (right)

Butter 8-cup mold. Cut cake into ½-inch slices; cut slices into 1-inch strips. Place strips on bottom and side of mold, cutting strips to fit.

Mix sugar, salt, egg yolks and gelatin in 3-quart saucepan; gradually stir in milk. Cook over medium heat, stirring constantly, just to boiling (do not boil). Place saucepan in ice and water, stirring occasionally, until mixture mounds slightly when dropped from a spoon. (If mixture looks slightly curdled, beat with wire whisk.) Beat whipping cream and vanilla in chilled medium bowl until stiff. Fold gelatin mixture into whipped cream mixture. Pour into cake-lined mold.

Cover and refrigerate at least 8 hours or until firm. Prepare Apricot Sauce. Unmold dessert onto large serving plate. Serve with Apricot Sauce. Refrigerate any remaining dessert. **8 to 10 servings.**

Apricot Sauce

4 ounces dried apricots (about ⅔ cup)
1 cup orange juice
½ cup sugar

Mix apricots and orange juice in 1½-quart saucepan. Heat to boiling; reduce heat. Cover and simmer about 20 minutes or until apricots are tender. Pour into blender or food processor. Cover and blend until of uniform consistency. Return mixture to saucepan; stir in sugar. Cook over medium heat about 2 minutes, stirring occasionally, or until sugar is completely dissolved; cool.

Dessert Wine Jelly

Wine jelly has been an American favorite since the nineteenth century.

4 envelopes unflavored gelatin
2 cups cold water
3 cups white or red grape juice
1 cup sugar
1 cup medium dry white wine
Sweetened whipped cream

Sprinkle gelatin on cold water in medium bowl to soften. Heat grape juice to boiling. Stir grape juice and sugar into gelatin mixture until gelatin is dissolved. Stir in wine. Pour into 6-cup mold. Refrigerate about 4 hours or until firm. Unmold onto serving plate. Serve with whipped cream. **12 servings.**

Chocolate Chiffon Icebox Cake

3 tablespoons hot water
1 bar (4 ounces) sweet cooking chocolate
1 envelope unflavored gelatin
3 tablespoons cold water
1 cup milk, scalded
½ cup powdered sugar
1 teaspoon vanilla
½ Burnt Sugar Chiffon Cake (page 39)
1½ cups whipping (heavy) cream

Heat hot water and chocolate over low heat, stirring constantly, until chocolate is melted. Cool to room temperature.

Sprinkle gelatin on cold water in medium bowl to soften. Stir in hot milk, powdered sugar and vanilla; stir until gelatin is completely dissolved. Refrigerate about 45 minutes, stirring occasionally, until mixture is partially set.

Cut cake into ½-inch slices; cut slices into 1-inch strips. Place strips on bottom and sides of loaf pan, 9 × 5 × 3 inches. Beat whipping cream in chilled medium bowl until stiff. Fold in chocolate mixture with wire whisk. Fold in gelatin mixture. Pour into cake-lined pan.

Cover and refrigerate about 5 hours or until firm. Unmold onto serving plate. Garnish with whipped cream if desired. Refrigerate any remaining dessert. **8 to 10 servings.**

Strawberry Crown

½ cup all-purpose flour
¼ cup chopped pecans or walnuts
¼ cup butter or margarine, softened
2 tablespoons packed brown sugar
1 envelope unflavored gelatin
½ cup cold water
1 quart strawberries, cut lengthwise into fourths
¾ cup granulated sugar
1 teaspoon lemon juice
Few drops red food color
1 cup whipping (heavy) cream

Heat oven to 400°. Mix flour, pecans, butter and brown sugar until crumbly. Spread in ungreased square pan, 9 × 9 × 2 inches. Bake 12 to 15 minutes or until golden brown. Stir to break up.

Sprinkle gelatin on cold water to soften. Mash 1 cup of the strawberries in 1½-quart saucepan. Stir in granulated sugar and lemon juice. Heat to boiling over medium heat, stirring occasionally; remove from heat. Stir in gelatin until dissolved. Stir in food color. Pour ¼ cup of the gelatin mixture into 7-cup mold. Arrange a few strawberry fourths, cut sides up, on gelatin mixture. Refrigerate until firm. Refrigerate remaining gelatin mixture about 40 minutes, stirring occasionally, until slightly thickened.

Beat whipping cream in chilled medium bowl until stiff. Fold in remaining strawberries and slightly thickened gelatin mixture. Alternate layers of whipped cream mixture and crumb mixture in mold, beginning with whipped cream mixture and ending with crumbs. Refrigerate about 3 hours or until firm. Unmold onto serving plate. Refrigerate any remaining dessert. **10 to 12 servings.**

Boysenberry-Apple Crumb Dessert

1½ cups crushed vanilla wafers
¼ cup butter or margarine, melted
½ cup butter or margarine, softened
1 cup powdered sugar
1 cup fresh boysenberries*
1 medium unpared eating apple, chopped
1 can (8 ounces) crushed pineapple, well drained
¾ cup whipping (heavy) cream
1 tablespoon powdered sugar

Mix wafer crumbs and melted butter; reserve ½ cup. Press remaining crumb mixture firmly in ungreased square, 8 × 8 × 2 or 9 × 9 × 2 inches. Beat softened butter on medium speed until light and fluffy; beat in 1 cup powdered sugar on low speed. Spread evenly over crumb mixture.

Mix boysenberries, apple and pineapple. Spoon evenly over butter mixture; press lightly into butter mixture. Beat whipping cream and 1 tablespoon powdered sugar in chilled small bowl until stiff; spread over fruit mixture.

Sprinkle reserved crumbs over top. Cover and refrigerate at least 8 hours. Refrigerate any remaining dessert. **9 servings.**

1 cup frozen boysenberries, thawed and drained, can be substituted for the fresh boysenberries.

Cranberry Refrigerator Dessert

1 cup sugar
¾ cup water
1 package (12 ounces) frozen cranberries (3 cups)
1 teaspoon grated orange peel
2 cups whipping (heavy) cream
¼ cup powdered sugar
1 cup finely crushed saltine cracker crumbs (24 to 30 crackers)
¼ cup chopped nuts

Heat 1 cup sugar and the water to boiling, stirring occasionally. Stir in cranberries. Heat to boiling; reduce heat, cook over low heat about 10 minutes or until cranberries pop; remove from heat. Stir in orange peel. Cool about 1 hour or until room temperature.

Beat whipping cream and powdered sugar in chilled bowl until soft peaks form. Spread ½ cup crumbs in clear glass 8-cup bowl. Spoon about 1⅓ cups whipped cream mixture in small dollops over crumbs; spread carefully. Spoon ¾ cup cranberry mixture over whipped cream. Repeat twice. Sprinkle with nuts. Cover and refrigerate 4 hours or until set. Serve with additional whipped cream if desired. **8 servings.**

Coconut Icebox Dessert

1/3 cup sugar
2 tablespoons cornstarch
1/8 teaspoon salt
2 cups milk
2 egg yolks, slightly beaten
2 tablespoons butter or margarine, softened
1 teaspoon vanilla
1 cup whipping (heavy) cream
2 cups coarsely chopped vanilla wafers
1/2 cup chopped walnuts
3/4 cup toasted coconut

Mix sugar, cornstarch and salt in 2-quart saucepan. Gradually stir in milk. Cook over medium heat, stirring constantly, until mixture thickens and boils. Boil and stir 1 minute. Stir at least half of the hot mixture gradually into egg yolks; stir into hot mixture in saucepan. Boil and stir 1 minute; remove from heat. Stir in butter and vanilla. Pour into large bowl. Place waxed paper or plastic wrap directly on surface. Refrigerate about 1 hour or until cool.

Stir pudding slightly, if necessary, to soften. Beat whipping cream in chilled bowl until stiff. Fold whipped cream, vanilla wafers, walnuts and 1/2 cup of the coconut into pudding. Spoon into 6-cup bowl. Sprinkle with remaining coconut and, if desired, candied cherries. Cover and refrigerate 2 hours or until set. Serve with additional whipped cream if desired. **6 servings.**

Peppermint Angel Food Dessert

This recipe is perfect if you have leftover Angel Food Cake Deluxe (page 37). You can also use a cake made from a packaged mix or a store-bought cake with delicious results!

1/4 cup sugar
1/4 cup crushed peppermint candies
1 tablespoon cornstarch
Dash of salt
1 cup milk
1 egg yolk, slightly beaten
4 or 5 drops red food color
1 cup whipping (heavy) cream
About 1/2 angel food cake

Mix sugar, candies, cornstarch and salt in 1½-quart saucepan. Gradually stir in milk. Cook over medium heat, stirring constantly, until mixture thickens and boils. Boil and stir 1 minute. Stir at least half of the hot mixture gradually into egg yolk; stir into hot mixture in saucepan. Boil and stir 1 minute; remove from heat. Stir in food color. Refrigerate about 15 minutes, stirring occasionally, until mixture mounds slightly when dropped from a spoon.

Beat whipping cream in chilled large bowl until stiff. Fold peppermint mixture into whipped cream. Tear enough angel food cake into about 1½-inch pieces to measure 6 cups. Fold into peppermint mixture.

Spoon into ungreased square baking dish, 8 × 8 × 2 inches. Cover and refrigerate at least 2 hours or until set. Cut into squares. Serve with additional whipped cream and crushed peppermint candy if desired. **9 servings.**

Orange Mallow

*22 large marshmallows or 2 cups miniature
    marshmallows*
1 teaspoon grated orange peel
²/₃ cup orange juice
1 cup whipping (heavy) cream

Heat marshmallows, orange peel and orange juice
over medium heat, stirring constantly, until marshmallows are melted. Cool about 15 minutes, or
until thickened.

Beat whipping cream in chilled medium bowl
until stiff. Stir marshmallow mixture to blend.
Fold into whipped cream. Divide among 6 dessert dishes. Refrigerate about 2 hours or until
set. Refrigerate any remaining dessert. **6 servings.**

Chocolate Pudding Parfaits

Chocolate Pudding (page 75)
1 cup whipping (heavy) cream
1 tablespoon powdered sugar
*1 cup flaked or shredded coconut, toasted
    (see Note, page 26)*
1 to 1½ cups sliced fresh fruit

Prepare Chocolate Pudding—except do not pour
into dessert dishes. Place waxed paper or plastic
wrap directly on surface of pudding. Refrigerate
until chilled.

Beat whipping cream and powdered sugar in
chilled small bowl until stiff. Alternate layers of
pudding, coconut, fruit and whipped cream in 6
parfait glasses. (Make 2 layers of each.) Refrigerate until chilled. **6 servings.**

Ginger-Cream Parfaits

1½ cups whipping (heavy) cream
2 tablespoons powdered sugar
*1 cup gingersnap crumbs, about 8 cookies
    (page 112)*

Beat whipping cream and powered sugar in chilled
medium bowl until stiff. Layer crumbs and
whipped cream in 4 parfait glasses, beginning
with crumbs and ending with whipped cream.
(Make about 4 layers of each.) Refrigerate at
least 5 hours but no longer than 24 hours. **4
servings.**

In nineteenth century America, food
preparation was revolutionized by the introduction of the icebox. A chunk of ice,
delivered by the iceman in a horse-drawn
cart, cooled the air in the icebox. When it
melted, it was replaced by a fresh chunk of
ice. With the introduction of the icebox, and
later the refrigerator and freezer, came new
types of recipes. Often one of these new
"icebox desserts" such as Boysenberry-Apple
Crumb Dessert and Peppermint Angel Food
Dessert took just a few minutes of preparation time. Then the refrigerator would do the
rest of the work by allowing the ingredients to
set up as they chilled. This kind of no-fuss
convenience cooking was a popular trend in
post-war America.

Individual Lime Schaum Tortes

A schaum torte may be either an unadorned meringue or a more complicated dessert resembling an angel pie (page 55). These pretty little tortes have appeared in different versions in Betty Crocker cookbooks through the years, dating all the way back to the first *Betty Crocker's Cookbook*, published in 1950.

Meringue Shells (right)
¾ cup sugar
3 tablespoons cornstarch
⅛ teaspoon salt
¾ cup water
3 egg yolks, slightly beaten
1 tablespoon butter or margarine
1 tablespoon grated lime peel
⅓ cup lime juice
Few drops green food color
1 cup whipping (heavy) cream

Prepare Meringue Shells. Mix sugar, cornstarch and salt in 1½-quart saucepan. Gradually stir in water. Cook over medium heat, stirring constantly, until mixture thickens and boils. Boil and stir 1 minute. Stir at least half of the hot mixture gradually into egg yolks. Blend into hot mixture in saucepan. Boil and stir 1 minute; remove from heat. Stir in butter, lime peel, lime juice and food color. Cool 15 minutes; refrigerate until room temperature. Spoon into shells. Cover and refrigerate at least 12 hours.

Beat whipping cream in chilled small bowl until stiff. Spread over filling. Refrigerate any remaining tortes. **6 servings.**

Meringue Shells

3 egg whites
¼ teaspoon cream of tartar
¾ cup sugar

Heat oven to 275°. Cover cookie sheet with heavy brown paper. Beat egg whites and cream of tartar in medium bowl on high speed until foamy. Beat in sugar, 1 tablespoon at a time; continue beating until stiff and glossy. Do not underbeat. Shape meringue on brown paper into six 3½-inch circles with back of spoon, building up sides. Bake 45 minutes. Turn off oven; leave meringues in oven with door closed 1 hour. Remove from oven; finish cooling meringues away from draft.

Layered Fruit Dessert

This simple dessert is especially pretty served with whipped cream and garnished with lightly toasted sliced or slivered almonds.

3 cups 1-inch cake pieces
2 cups cut-up fresh fruit
Creamy Stirred Custard (page 64)

Layer cake and fruit in 6 dessert dishes. Top with Creamy Stirred Custard. Cover and refrigerate about 2 hours or until chilled. **6 servings.**

Individual Lime Schaum Torte, Strawberry Crown (page 81)

Icy Coffee Cream

1 envelope unflavored gelatin
¼ cup cold water
1½ cups strong coffee
¼ cup packed brown sugar
1½ cups whipping (heavy) cream
¼ cup powdered sugar
½ teaspoon vanilla

Sprinkle gelatin on cold water in 1½-quart saucepan to soften. Stir in coffee and brown sugar. Heat over low heat, stirring constantly, until gelatin is dissolved. Place saucepan in bowl of ice and water about 10 minutes, or refrigerate about 30 minutes, stirring occasionally, just until mixture mounds slightly when dropped from spoon.

Beat whipping cream, powdered sugar and vanilla in chilled medium bowl until stiff. Fold coffee mixture into whipped cream. Pour into square pan, 8 × 8 × 2 inches. Cover and freeze at least 8 hours or until firm. Let stand 10 minutes before serving. **8 to 10 servings.**

Frozen Torte

4 egg whites
½ teaspoon cream of tartar
1 cup sugar
Mocha Filling (below)

Heat oven to 275°. Cover 2 cookie sheets with heavy brown paper. Beat egg whites and cream of tartar in large bowl on high speed until foamy. Beat in sugar, 1 tablespoon at a time; continue beating until stiff and glossy. Do not underbeat.

Divide meringue into 3 parts. Place 1 part on 1 cookie sheet; shape into 6-inch circle. Place remaining 2 parts on second cookie sheet; shape each part into 6-inch circle. Bake 45 minutes. Turn off oven; leave meringues in oven with door closed 1 hour. Remove from oven; finish cooling meringues away from draft.

Stack meringues, spreading Mocha Filling between layers; frost top of torte with filling. Decorate with shaved chocolate if desired. Freeze uncovered at least 3 hours or until filling on top is firm. (For ease in cutting, dip knife into hot water and wipe after cutting each slice.) **6 servings.**

Mocha Filling

¼ cup sugar
3 tablespoons cocoa
2 tablespoons powdered instant coffee
2 cups whipping (heavy) cream

Beat all ingredients in chilled medium bowl until stiff.

Peach Ice Cream

½ cup sugar
1 cup milk
¼ teaspoon salt
3 egg yolks, beaten
2 cups whipping (heavy) cream
1 tablespoon vanilla
2 cups peeled mashed peaches (4 to 5 medium)
½ cup sugar

Mix ½ cup sugar, the milk, salt and egg yolks in 1-quart saucepan. Cook over medium heat, stirring constantly, just to boiling (do not boil). Refrigerate uncovered in chilled bowl 1 to 1½ hours or until room temperature.

Stir whipping cream and vanilla into milk mixture. Mix peaches and ½ cup sugar; stir into cream mixture. Pour into 1-quart ice-cream freezer. Freeze according to manufacturers' directions. **About 1 quart ice cream.**

Apple Ice Cream

½ cup sugar
1 cup milk
¼ teaspoon salt
3 egg yolks, beaten
2 cups whipping (heavy) cream
1 teaspoon vanilla
3 or 4 drops red or green food color, if desired
3 medium eating apples, pared, cored and cut up
½ cup sugar
1 tablespoon lemon juice

Mix ½ cup sugar, the milk, salt and egg yolks in 1-quart saucepan. Cook over medium heat, stirring constantly, just to boiling (do not boil). Refrigerate uncovered in chilled bowl 1 to 1½ hours or until room temperature.

Stir whipping cream, vanilla and food color into milk mixture. Place half of the apples, ½ cup sugar and the lemon juice in food processor or blender. Cover and process, using quick on-and-off motions, until coarsely chopped. Add remaining apples.

Cover and process until finely chopped but not mashed. Stir into milk mixture. Pour into 2-quart ice-cream freezer. Freeze according to manufacturers' directions. **About 1½ quarts ice cream.**

Apple Ice Cream, Cinnamon Cake (page 33)

Caramel Crunch Ice Cream

You will certainly taste the southern influence in this special ice cream. The mix of Caramel Crunch and pecans imitates the flavor of a southern favorite, the praline. Like this ice cream, pralines are made with brown sugar and pecans.

½ cup sugar
1 cup milk
¼ teaspoon salt
3 egg yolks, beaten
Caramel Crunch (below)
½ cup chopped pecans
2 cups whipping (heavy) cream
1 tablespoon vanilla

Mix sugar, milk, salt and egg yolks in 1½-quart saucepan. Heat over medium heat, stirring constantly, just to boiling (do not boil). Refrigerate uncovered in chilled bowl at least 2 hours.

Prepare Caramel Crunch. Stir Caramel Crunch, pecans, whipping cream and vanilla into milk mixture. Pour into 1-quart ice-cream freezer. Freeze according to manufacturers' directions. **About 1 quart ice cream.**

Caramel Crunch

1 tablespoon butter or margarine, softened
⅓ cup packed brown sugar

Spread butter on cookie sheet, 15½ × 12 inches, leaving 1½-inch border on all sides. Sprinkle brown sugar evenly over buttered area. Set oven control to broil. Broil 3 to 4 inches from heat 1 to 2 minutes or until brown sugar is melted. (Watch closely as mixture burns quickly.) Cool slightly; remove from cookie sheet with spatula. Break into pieces.

Marco Polo is rumored to have brought back a recipe for an ice cream confection from Asia, but ice cream did not become widely known in Europe until the late seventeenth century. Ice cream became popular in the American colonies toward the end of the next century—it seems that even George Washington was quite fond of it! Ice cream in Europe was made with a custard base. Philadelphia, the birthplace of our Constitution, was also the birthplace of a special American kind of ice cream. Made without egg custard, Philadelphia Ice Cream is both rich and simple. First Lady Dolley Madison, who served ice cream frequently at the White House, is credited with making ice cream the popular American treat it remains today.

Philadelphia Ice Cream

½ cup sugar
3 cups whipping (heavy) cream
4½ teaspoons vanilla
⅛ teaspoon salt

Mix all ingredients until sugar is dissolved. Pour into 1-quart ice-cream freezer. Freeze according to manufacturers' directions. **About 1 quart ice cream.**

Buttermilk Sherbet

1 cup sugar
2 cups buttermilk
¼ cup lemon juice
1 teaspoon grated lemon peel

Mix all ingredients until sugar is dissolved. Pour into 1-quart ice-cream freezer. Freeze according to manufacturers' directions. **About 1 quart sherbet.**

Fresh Lemon Sherbet

1¼ cups sugar
2 cups half-and-half
⅓ cup lemon juice
1 to 2 tablespoons lemon peel
1 or 2 drops yellow food color

Mix all ingredients until sugar is dissolved. Pour into 1-quart ice-cream freezer. Freeze according to manufacturers' directions. **About 1 quart sherbet.**

Three-Fruit Ice

1 cup sugar
⅛ teaspoon salt
1¼ cups water
½ cup orange juice (1 medium orange)
3 tablespoons lemon juice (1 lemon)
2 ripe bananas, mashed (about ¾ cup)

Heat sugar, salt and half of the water to boiling in 1-quart saucepan; remove from heat. Stir in remaining water, orange juice, lemon juice and bananas. Pour into 1-quart ice-cream freezer. Freeze according to manufacturers' directions. **About 1 quart ice.**

CHAPTER SIX

Homespun Pastries and Cookies

Delicious, melt-in-your-mouth pastries and freshly baked cookies bring up warm memories of lunch-box treats, midnight snacks and cozy winter afternoons. We all have a favorite pastry or cookie, be it a custard-filled éclair, a flaky strudel, a soft and chewy bar or a crisp refrigerator cookie. You can be certain that a full cookie jar won't stay that way for long.

Cookies are wonderful because they're fun and simple to make. They are also easy to shape into different forms and decorate, which makes them perfect for holidays and other special days. Invite friends to a cookie trading party, a lovely holiday tradition; everyone brings a batch of home-baked cookies and leaves with a sampling of everyone else's.

Icebox cookies have been long-time favorites because they're so convenient. You can make the dough when you have free time, and then slice and bake them as needed. Warm and delicious, these cookies will be ready in minutes. You can refrigerate the rolls of dough for several weeks, or freeze them in moisture-proof and vaporproof wrapping for up to a year.

Children love to make and serve cookies. Whether they're icebox cookies, chewy bars or elegant rolled cookies, children and adults alike will enjoy shaping and decorating their own cookies. But the best part of making cookies, of course, is eating them up!

Cream-filled Horns (page 96), Peppermint Pinwheels
(page 101), Sand Tarts (page 110)   95

Cream-filled Horns

1 cup firm butter or margarine
1½ cups all-purpose flour
½ cup sour cream
½ cup granulated sugar
3 tablespoons water
1½ cups whipping (heavy) cream
⅓ cup powdered sugar

Cut butter into flour in medium bowl until pastry gathers together and forms a soft ball. Stir in sour cream. Divide dough in half. Wrap each half and refrigerate at least 8 hours.

Heat oven to 350°. Cover cookie sheet with cooking parchment paper, or lightly grease cookie sheet. Mix granulated sugar and water. Roll one half of the pastry into rectangle, 16 × 12 inches, on well-floured cloth-covered surface (keep other half refrigerated). Brush with sugar mixture. Cut lengthwise into twelve 1-inch strips. Being careful not to stretch pastry, wrap 2 strips, glazed sides out, around each cream horn mold, overlapping ½ inch with each turn. Place on cookie sheet. Bake about 25 minutes or until golden brown. Immediately remove from cookie sheet. Cool slightly before removing from molds.

Repeat with other half of pastry. Beat whipping cream and powdered sugar in chilled medium bowl until stiff. Fill horns with whipped cream. **12 horns.**

Note: To make cream horn molds, cut double-thickness heavy-duty aluminum foil into 8-inch squares. Fold each into triangle; roll into cone shape.

Cream Puffs

1 cup water
½ cup butter or margarine
1 cup all-purpose flour
4 eggs
Fillings (below)

Heat oven to 400°. Heat water and butter to rolling boil in 2½-quart saucepan. Stir in flour; reduce heat. Stir vigorously over low heat about 1 minute or until mixture forms a ball; remove from heat. Beat in eggs, all at once; continue beating until smooth. Drop dough by scant ¼ cupfuls 3 inches apart onto ungreased cookie sheet.

Bake 35 to 40 minutes or until puffed and golden. Cool away from draft. Cut off top one-third of each puff; pull out any filaments of soft dough. Fill puffs with one of the Fillings; replace tops. Serve immediately or cover and refrigerate no longer than 4 hours. **10 to 12 cream puffs.**

Peppermint Whipped Cream Filling

2 cups whipping (heavy) cream
¼ cup sugar
1 teaspoon peppermint extract
5 or 6 drops red or green food color

Beat ingredients in chilled medium bowl until stiff.

Coffee Whipped Cream Filling

2 cups whipping (heavy) cream
1½ teaspoons instant coffee

Beat ingredients in chilled medium bowl until stiff.

Eclairs

1 cup water
½ cup butter or margarine
1 cup all-purpose flour
4 eggs
Cream Filling (below)
Chocolate Frosting (right)

Heat oven to 400°. Heat water and butter to rolling boil in 2½-quart saucepan. Stir in flour; reduce heat. Stir vigorously over low heat about 1 minute or until mixture forms a ball; remove from heat. Beat in eggs, all at once; continue beating until smooth. Drop dough by scant ¼ cupfuls 3 inches apart onto ungreased cookie sheet. Shape each into finger 4½ inches long and 1½ inches wide with spatula.

Bake 35 to 40 minutes or until puffed and golden. Cool away from draft. Cut off top third of each éclair; pull out any filaments of soft dough. Prepare Cream Filling. Fill éclairs with filling; replace tops. Frost with Chocolate Frosting just before serving. Serve immediately or cover and refrigerate no longer than 4 hours. **10 to 12 éclairs.**

Cream Filling

⅓ cup sugar
2 tablespoons cornstarch
⅛ teaspoon salt
2 cups milk
2 egg yolks, slightly beaten
2 tablespoons margarine or butter, softened
2 teaspoons vanilla

Mix sugar, cornstarch and salt in 2-quart saucepan. Gradually stir in milk. Cook over medium heat, stirring constantly, until mixture thickens and boils. Boil and stir 1 minute. Gradually stir at least half of the hot mixture into egg yolks. Stir into hot mixture in saucepan. Boil and stir 1 minute; remove from heat. Stir in margarine and vanilla; cool.

Chocolate Frosting

¾ cup semisweet chocolate chips
2 tablespoons butter or margarine
1 tablespoon corn syrup

Heat all ingredients over low heat, stirring constantly, until chocolate is melted; cool.

DESSERTS THEN

Puff pastry has been used in many dessert recipes since at least the seventeenth century—some say as far back as the thirteenth century. And for just as long it has been considered difficult and time-consuming to make. The butter-rich dough must be rolled and folded many times in order to achieve puff pastry's celebrated flaky, light texture. While pastry chefs seem inclined to make their own puff pastry, most of us use shortcut recipes that are faster and easier to prepare. Cream-filled Horns, for example, get their flaky texture from the sour cream used in the dough. Another delicious and practical way to have the luxury of flaky pastry is using frozen phyllo dough (as in Pear-Fig Strudel).

Pear~Fig Strudel with Eggnog Sauce

Be sure to prepare the pear-fig filling first, to ensure that the phyllo dough doesn't dry out. If you are using butter to brush the phyllo, use unsalted or lightly salted butter; too much salt in the butter can cause brown speckles to appear on the surface of the baked pastry.

2 pounds ripe pears, pared and coarsely chopped (about 4 large)

1 teaspoon grated lemon peel

2 tablespoons lemon juice

½ cup coarsely chopped pistachios

⅓ to ½ cup sugar

½ teaspoon ground cinnamon

¼ teaspoon ground ginger

⅛ teaspoon ground cloves

1 package (8 ounces) dried figs, stems removed and cut in half

⅓ cup unseasoned dry bread crumbs

Eggnog Sauce (right)

6 frozen phyllo sheets, thawed

½ cup butter or margarine, melted

Powdered sugar, if desired

Heat pears, lemon peel and lemon juice in 10-inch skillet over medium heat about 5 minutes, stirring occasionally, until pears are soft; remove from heat. Stir in pistachios, sugar, cinnamon, ginger, cloves and figs, mixing well. Stir in bread crumbs. Prepare Eggnog Sauce.

Heat oven to 400°. Line jelly roll pan, 15½ × 10½ × 1 inch, with cooking parchment paper or aluminum foil. Place damp towel on work surface, long side facing you. Cover with plastic wrap or waxed paper. Place phyllo sheets on plastic wrap. Cover with plastic wrap. Fold sheets crosswise in half. Unfold sheets one at a time, brushing each with butter. Repeat with other side. Spread pear-fig mixture evenly over bottom third of pastry, leaving 2-inch border. Fold in 2-inch border on all sides. Fold into thirds, using plastic wrap to help fold. Place seam side down diagonally in pan. Brush with butter. Bake about 30 minutes, brushing with butter every 10 minutes, until golden brown. Cool slightly; dust with powdered sugar. Cut into slices to serve. Serve with Eggnog Sauce. 8 to 10 servings.

Eggnog Sauce

2 cups prepared eggnog

1 tablespoon cornstarch

Mix eggnog and cornstarch with wire whisk in 2-quart saucepan. Heat over medium heat, stirring constantly, until boiling. Boil and stir 1 minute or until slightly thickened. Cover and refrigerate about 1 hour or until chilled.

Pear-Fig Strudel with Eggnog Sauce, Cream Puffs (page 96)

Petticoat Tails

How did these perfectly normal icebox cookies come by such an unusual name? The voice of Betty Crocker offered a few possible explanations on "Betty Crocker's Cooking School of the Air" in 1937. Our favorite is this one: "This recipe was brought from France to Scotland by Mary, Queen of Scots. The French name was *petits gateaux tailles* (translated as 'little cakes cut off'). But as happened with many of the French terms that the English could not pronounce correctly, the name was corrupted, and they were called as they *sounded* to the Scotch or English ear: 'petticoat tails.' "

1 cup powdered sugar
1 cup butter or margarine, softened
2½ cups all-purpose flour
¼ teaspoon salt
1 teaspoon vanilla or ½ teaspoon almond extract

Mix powdered sugar and butter in medium bowl. Stir in remaining ingredients, using hands if necessary. Shape dough into roll about 9 inches long. Wrap and refrigerate at least 2 hours.

Heat oven to 400°. Cut roll into ⅛-inch slices. Place slices about 1 inch apart on ungreased cookie sheet. Bake 6 to 8 minutes or until light brown. Cool slightly; remove from cookie sheet. **About 6 dozen cookies.**

Oatmeal Refrigerator Cookies

½ cup granulated sugar
½ cup packed brown sugar
½ cup butter or margarine, softened
2 tablespoons molasses
1½ teaspoons grated lemon peel
½ teaspoon vanilla
1 egg
1½ cups all-purpose flour
1½ cups quick-cooking or regular oats
½ teaspoon baking soda
¼ teaspoon salt

Mix sugars, butter, molasses, lemon peel, vanilla and egg in large bowl. Stir in remaining ingredients (dough will be stiff). Shape into roll about 15 inches long. Wrap and refrigerate at least 3 hours.

Heat oven to 375°. Cut roll into ¼-inch slices. Place slices 2 inches apart on ungreased cookie sheet. Bake 7 to 9 minutes or until edges begin to brown. **About 5 dozen cookies.**

Peppermint Pinwheels

1 cup powdered sugar
1 cup butter or margarine, softened
1½ teaspoons almond extract
1 teaspoon vanilla
1 egg
2½ cups all-purpose flour
½ teaspoon salt
¼ teaspoon red food color
Granulated sugar
Glaze (below)
¼ cup finely crushed peppermint candy

Mix powdered sugar, butter, almond extract, vanilla and egg in medium bowl. Stir in flour and salt. Divide dough in half. Stir food color into one half until evenly covered. Cover and refrigerate 1 hour or until firm.

Roll each half into 8-inch square on lightly floured cloth-covered surface. Place red square on plain square. Roll into 12-inch square. Roll up tightly. Wrap and refrigerate 2 hours or until firm.

Heat oven to 375°. Cut rolls into ⅛-inch slices. Place slices about 1 inch apart on ungreased cookie sheet. Sprinkle lightly with granulated sugar. Bake 7 to 9 minutes or until light brown. Spread warm cookies with thin layer of Glaze; immediately sprinkle with crushed peppermint candy. **About 8 dozen cookies.**

Glaze

1 cup powdered sugar
1 tablespoon corn syrup
3½ teaspoons warm water

Mix all ingredients until smooth.

Cookies have been favorite American treats since the first colonists landed here. The Pennsylvania Dutch called them *koekje* (pronounced "cookie"), and somehow this name stuck. Often cookies were baked as little cakes more to test the heat of the oven than as a separate recipe. Baking cookies has long been a special activity, especially around Christmas. Many immigrants brought recipes and cookie cutters with them from the old country and made fancy cookies for holiday celebrations. From simple drop cookies, to easy refrigerator cookies, to hearty bars, cookies are still one of the best treats we can imagine, no matter what the occasion.

Sour Cream–Nut Cookies

1 cup sugar
⅓ cup butter or margarine, softened
¼ cup shortening
1 teaspoon vanilla
1 egg
2⅔ cups all-purpose flour
½ cup finely chopped nuts, toasted (see Note, page 26)
⅔ cup sour cream
1 teaspoon baking powder
½ teaspoon baking soda
½ teaspoon salt
Sugar

Heat oven to 375°. Mix sugar, butter, shortening, vanilla and egg in large bowl. Stir in remaining ingredients.

Shape dough into 1½-inch balls. Place about 2 inches apart on ungreased cookie sheet. Flatten each with greased bottom of glass dipped into sugar. Bake 7 to 8 minutes or until almost no imprint remains when touched. **About 3 dozen cookies.**

Gingersnaps

1 cup sugar
¾ cup shortening
¼ cup dark molasses
1 egg
2¼ cups all-purpose flour
1 tablespoon ground ginger
1½ teaspoons baking soda
1 teaspoon ground cinnamon
¼ teaspoon salt
Sugar

Mix 1 cup sugar, the shortening, molasses and egg in medium bowl. Stir in remaining ingredients except sugar. Cover and refrigerate at least 1 hour.

Heat oven to 375°. Shape dough into 1-inch balls; dip tops into sugar. Place balls, sugared sides up, about 3 inches apart on ungreased cookie sheet. Bake 10 to 12 minutes or until edges are set (centers will be soft). **About 4½ dozen cookies.**

Gingersnaps, Old-time Cinnamon Jumbles (page 104)

Lemon-Ginger Crinkles

1 cup packed brown sugar
½ cup shortening
1 egg
1 tablespoon grated lemon peel
1½ cups all-purpose flour
½ teaspoon baking soda
½ teaspoon cream of tartar
¼ teaspoon salt
¼ teaspoon ground ginger
Granulated sugar

Heat oven to 350°. Mix brown sugar, shortening, egg and lemon peel in large bowl. Stir in flour, baking soda, cream of tartar, salt and ginger.

Shape dough into 1-inch balls; dip tops into granulated sugar. Place balls, sugared sides up about 3 inches apart on ungreased cookie sheet. Bake 10 to 11 minutes or until almost no indentation remains when touched. **About 4 dozen cookies.**

Old-time Cinnamon Jumbles

"Betty Crocker's Cooking School of the Air" devoted a segment to these same Old-time Cinnamon Jumbles back in the winter of 1938. The voice of Betty Crocker said, "Now these cinnamon jumbles are like an old-time soft sugar cookie, with the extra touch of a sprinkling of fragrant cinnamon and sugar on top. And I hope that all the radio friends who asked me in the past about a really soft, thick, old-fashioned white cookie, are listening in so they'll be able to get this recipe." If you weren't listening back in 1938, here's the recipe one more time.

¼ cup sugar
1 teaspoon ground cinnamon
1 cup sugar
½ cup butter or margarine, softened
1 egg
¾ cup buttermilk
1 teaspoon vanilla
2 cups all-purpose flour
½ teaspoon baking soda
¼ teaspoon salt

Heat oven to 400°. Mix ¼ cup sugar and the cinnamon; reserve. Mix 1 cup sugar, the butter and egg in medium bowl. Stir in buttermilk and vanilla. Stir in flour, baking soda and salt. Drop dough by rounded teaspoonfuls about 2 inches apart onto ungreased cookie sheet. Sprinkle with cinnamon-sugar mixture. Bake 8 to 10 minutes or until set but not brown. **About 4½ dozen cookies.**

Chocolate Drop Cookies

Chocolate drop cookies appeared in the first *Betty Crocker's Cookbook*. Easy and quick to make, they've been favorites for years.

1 cup sugar
½ cup butter or margarine, softened
1 egg
2 ounces unsweetened chocolate, melted and cooled
⅓ cups buttermilk or water
1 teaspoon vanilla
1¾ cup all-purpose flour
½ teaspoon baking soda
½ teaspoon salt
1 cup chopped nuts, if desired
Chocolate Frosting (below)

Heat oven to 400°. Mix sugar, butter, egg, chocolate, buttermilk and vanilla in medium bowl. Stir in flour, baking soda, salt and nuts. Drop dough by rounded teaspoonfuls about 2 inches apart onto ungreased cookie sheet.

Bake 8 to 10 minutes or until almost no indentation remains when touched. Immediately remove from cookie sheet; cool. Frost with Chocolate Frosting. **About 4½ dozen cookies.**

Chocolate Frosting

2 ounces unsweetened chocolate
2 tablespoons butter or margarine
3 tablespoons water
About 2 cups powdered sugar

Heat chocolate and butter in 1½-quart saucepan over low heat until melted; remove from heat. Stir in water and powdered sugar until smooth.

Banana-Spice Drops

¼ cup shortening
¼ cup butter or margarine, softened
2 eggs
1 cup packed brown sugar
1 cup mashed bananas (about 2 medium)
2 teaspoons baking powder
¼ teaspoon baking soda
¼ teaspoon salt
½ teaspoon ground cinnamon
¼ teaspoon ground cloves
2 cups all-purpose flour
½ cup chopped nuts
Cherry Frosting (below)

Mix shortening, butter, eggs, brown sugar, bananas, baking powder, baking soda, salt and spices thoroughly. Stir in flour and nuts. Cover and refrigerate at least 1 hour.

Heat oven to 375°. Drop dough by rounded teaspoonfuls about 2 inches apart onto lightly greased cookie sheet. Bake 8 to 10 minutes or until almost no indentation remains when touched. Immediately remove from cookie sheet; cool. Frost with Cherry Frosting. **About 4 dozen cookies.**

Cherry Frosting

3 cups powdered sugar
⅓ cup butter or margarine, softened
2 tablespoons drained chopped maraschino cherries
1½ teaspoons vanilla
2 drops red food color, if desired
About 2 tablespoons milk

Mix powdered sugar and butter. Stir in remaining ingredients until frosting is spreading consistency.

Almond-Cherry Macaroons

Almond macaroons are thought to have originated in Italy (where they are known as amaretti) in the sixteenth century. You can achieve their distinctively chewy insides complemented by crunchy outsides with surprisingly little time and effort.

1¼ cups coarsely chopped slivered almonds, toasted (see Note, page 26)
¾ cup sugar
3 egg whites
⅓ cup chopped maraschino cherries, well drained

Heat oven to 300°. Mix almonds, sugar and egg whites in 2-quart saucepan. Cook over medium heat about 6 minutes, stirring constantly, until a path remains when a spoon is drawn through mixture; remove from heat. Stir in cherries; cool slightly.

Cover cookie sheet with cooking parchment paper. Drop mixture by rounded teaspoonfuls about 1 inch apart onto parchment paper. Bake about 20 minutes or until light brown. Slide parchment paper and cookies onto wire rack; cool completely. Carefully remove cookies from paper. **About 3 dozen cookies.**

Coconut Meringues

4 egg whites
1¼ cups sugar
2½ cups coconut
½ teaspoon vanilla
¼ teaspoon salt

Heat oven to 325°. Lightly grease cookie sheet. Beat egg whites in medium bowl on high speed until foamy. Beat in sugar, 1 tablespoon at a time; continue beating until stiff and glossy. Do not underbeat. Fold in remaining ingredients. Drop mixture by heaping teaspoonfuls about 2 inches apart onto cookie sheet.

Bake about 20 minutes or until set and light brown. Immediately remove from cookie sheet; cool. Store in tightly covered container at room temperature no longer than 24 hours. **About 3 dozen cookies.**

Coconut Meringues, Butterscotch Sugar Cookies (page 108), Sour Cream-Nut Cookies (page 102)

Butterscotch Sugar Cookies

1 cup packed brown sugar
½ cup butter or margarine, softened
¼ cup shortening
1 teaspoon vanilla
2 eggs
2½ cups all-purpose flour
1 teaspoon baking powder
1 teaspoon salt
1 cup chopped black walnuts, if desired

Mix brown sugar, butter, shortening, vanilla and eggs in medium bowl. Blend in flour, baking powder and salt. Stir in walnuts. Cover and refrigerate at least 1 hour.

Heat oven to 400°. Roll dough ⅛ inch thick on lightly floured cloth-covered surface. Cut into desired shapes with 3-inch cookie cutters. Place on ungreased cookie sheet. Bake 6 to 8 minutes or until very light brown. Immediately remove from cookie sheet. **About 4 dozen cookies.**

Date-filled Turnovers

1 cup sugar
½ cup butter or margarine, softened
1 teaspoon vanilla
2 eggs
2½ cups all-purpose flour
½ teaspoon salt
¼ teaspoon baking soda
Date Filling (below)
Milk
Sugar

Mix 1 cup sugar, the butter, vanilla and eggs in medium bowl. Blend in flour, salt and baking soda. Cover and refrigerate 1 hour. While dough is chilling, prepare Date Filling.

Heat oven to 400°. Roll dough 1/16 inch thick on lightly floured cloth-covered surface. Cut into 3-inch circles or squares. Spoon 1 teaspoon filling on half of each circle. Fold dough over filling; press edges together.

Place 1 inch apart on ungreased cookie sheet. Brush with milk; sprinkle with sugar. Bake 8 to 10 minutes or until very light brown. Immediately remove from cookie sheet. **4½ dozen cookies.**

Date Filling

2 cups pitted dates, finely chopped
¾ cup sugar
½ cup chopped nuts, if desired
¾ cup water

Mix all ingredients in saucepan. Cook, stirring constantly, until mixture thickens; cool completely.

Date-filled Turnovers, Jam Bars (page 111)

Sand Tarts

These crisp rolled cookies have a "sandy" texture because coarse decorator's sugar is sprinkled on top. Originally, "granulated" sugar was obtained by pounding sugar blocks into coarse granules. That traditionally coarse texture is re-created today with decorator's sugar.

1 cup sugar
½ cup butter or margarine, softened
1 egg
1¾ cups all-purpose flour
⅓ cup finely chopped almonds
½ teaspoon baking soda
¼ teaspoon salt
1 egg white, beaten
3 tablespoons white decorator's sugar or granulated sugar
Ground cinnamon

Heat oven to 375°. Mix 1 cup sugar, the butter and egg in medium bowl. Stir in flour, almonds, baking soda and salt.

Divide dough into 3 equal parts. Roll each part ⅛ inch thick on lightly floured cloth-covered surface. Cut into desired shapes with 2- to 2½-inch cookie cutters. Brush cookies lightly with egg white; sprinkle with decorator's sugar. Sprinkle lightly with cinnamon. Place on ungreased cookie sheet. Bake 6 to 7 minutes or until edges are light brown. **About 5 dozen cookies.**

Apple Bars

1½ cups packed brown sugar
½ cup shortening
¼ cup milk
1 egg
2 cups all-purpose flour
1 teaspoon baking soda
1 teaspoon ground cinnamon
½ teaspoon ground nutmeg
¼ teaspoon ground cloves
2 cups chopped pared apples (about 2 medium)
1 cup chopped walnuts
Glaze (below)

Heat oven to 350°. Lightly grease rectangular pan, 13 × 9 × 2 inches. Mix brown sugar, shortening, milk and egg in large bowl. Stir in flour, baking soda, cinnamon, nutmeg and cloves; mix in apples and walnuts. Spread evenly in pan.

Bake 25 to 30 minutes or until toothpick inserted in center comes out clean. Cool 30 minutes; spread with Glaze. Cool completely; cut into 2 × 1½-inch bars. **36 bars.**

Glaze

1¼ cups powdered sugar
2 to 3 tablespoons milk

Mix ingredients until smooth and of spreading consistency.

Jam Bars

1 cup packed brown sugar
½ cup butter or margarine, softened
⅓ cup shortening
1¾ cups all-purpose flour
1½ cups quick-cooking oats
½ teaspoon salt
½ teaspoon baking soda
1 cup jam or preserves

Heat oven to 400°. Mix brown sugar, butter and shortening in medium bowl. Stir in remaining ingredients, except jam, until crumbly. Press half of the mixture in ungreased rectangular pan, 13 × 9 × 2 inches. Spread with jam. Top with remaining crumbly mixture; press lightly. Bake 25 to 30 minutes or until light brown. Cut into 2 × 1½-inch bars while warm. **36 bars.**

Walnut-Orange Bars

¾ cup powdered sugar
¼ cup cocoa
¾ cup butter or margarine, softened
1½ cups all-purpose flour
½ cup orange marmalade
1½ cups finely chopped walnuts
¾ cup packed brown sugar
¼ cup all-purpose flour
1 teaspoon vanilla
½ teaspoon baking powder
¼ teaspoon salt
2 eggs
Chocolate Glaze (right)

Heat oven to 375°. Mix powdered sugar, cocoa and butter; stir in 1½ cups flour. Press in ungreased rectangular pan, 13 × 9 × 2 inches. Bake about 10 minutes or just until edges begin to pull away from sides of pan.

Spread marmalade over baked layer. Mix remaining ingredients except glaze; spread over marmalade. Bake 20 to 25 minutes or until no indentation remains when touched in center; cool. Spread with Chocolate Glaze. Cut into 3 × 1-inch bars. **36 bars.**

Chocolate Glaze

3 tablespoons butter or margarine
1 tablespoon corn syrup
2 ounces unsweetened chocolate
1 cup powdered sugar
¾ teaspoon vanilla
About 2 tablespoons hot water

Heat butter, corn syrup and chocolate over low heat until melted; remove from heat. Stir in powdered sugar and vanilla. Beat in water, 1 teaspoon at a time, until smooth and of spreading consistency.

CANADIAN METRIC CONVERSION TABLES

Common Cooking & Baking Utensil Equivalents

Bakeware	Imperial	Metric
Round Pan	8 × 1½ inches	20 × 4 cm
	9 × 1½ inches	22 × 4 cm
Square Pan	8 × 8 × 2 inches	22 × 22 × 5 cm
	9 × 9 × 2 inches	23 × 23 × 5 cm
Baking Dishes	11 × 7 × 1½ inches	28 × 18 × 4 cm
	12 × 7½ × 2 inches	30 × 19 × 5 cm
	13 × 9 × 2 inches	33 × 23 × 5 cm
Loaf Pan	8½ × 4½ × 2½ inches	22 × 11 × 6 cm
	9 × 5 × 3 inches	23 × 13 × 8 cm
Tube Pan	10 × 4 inches	25 × 10 cm
Jelly Roll Pan	15½ × 10½ × 1 inch	39 × 27 × 2.5 cm
Pie Plate	9 × 1¼ inches	23 × 3.2 cm
	10 × 1½ inches	25 × 4 cm
Muffin Cups	2½ × 1¼ inches	6 × 3.2 cm
	3 × 1½ inches	8 × 4 cm
Skillet	10 inches	25 cm
Casseroles and Saucepans	1 quart	1 L
	1½ quarts	1.5 L
	2 quarts	2 L
	2½ quarts	2.5 L
	3 quarts	3 L
	4 quarts	4 L

Dry and Liquid Measurements

Imperial	Metric
¼ teaspoon	1 mL
½ teaspoon	2 mL
1 teaspoon	5 mL
1 tablespoon	15 mL
2 tablespoons	25 mL
3 tablespoons	50 mL
¼ cup	50 mL
⅓ cup	75 mL
½ cup	125 mL
⅔ cup	150 mL
¾ cup	175 mL
1 cup	250 mL

Temperatures

Fahrenheit	Celsius
32°F	0°C
212°F	100°C
250°F	121°C
275°F	140°C
300°F	150°C
325°F	160°C
350°F	180°C
375°F	190°C
400°F	200°C
425°F	220°C
450°F	230°C
475°F	240°C

Note: The recipes in this cookbook have not been developed or tested in Canadian metric measures. When converting to Canadian metric, some variations in recipe quality may be noted.

112

Index

Credits

Prentice Hall

Publisher: Nina Hoffman
Executive Editor: Rebecca W. Atwater
Editor: Anne Ficklen
Assistant Editor: Rachel Simon
Assistant Art Director: Frederick J. Latasa
Photographic Director and Props: Carmen Bonilla
Senior Production Manager: Susan Joseph
Assistant Managing Editor: Kimberly Ann Ebert

General Mills, Inc.

Editor: Cathy Swanson
Test Kitchen Home Economists: Mary H. Johnson, Linel Reiber
Recipe Copy Editor: Judy Lund
Editorial Assistant: Elaine Mitchell
Food Stylists: Mary Sethre, Kate Courtney, Cindy Lund
Photographer: Nanci Doonan Dixon
Photography Assistant: Valerie J. Bourassa
Director, Betty Crocker Food and Publications Center: Marcia Copeland
Assistant Manager, Publications: Lois Tlusty